Canoeing and Kayaking UTAH

The Utah Rivers Council holds a paddlefest every year.

Canoeing and Kayaking UTAH

A Complete Guide to Paddling Utah's Lakes, Reservoirs and Rivers

Michael R. Fine

THE COUNTRYMAN PRESS
A division of W. W. Norton & Company
Independent Publishers Since 1923

Copyright © 2006 by Michael R. Fine

First Edition

All rights reserved. No part of this book may be reproduced in any form by any electronic or mechanical means, including information storage and retrieval systems, without permission from the publisher, except by a reviewer, who may quote brief passages.

Library of Congress Cataloging-in-Publication Data has been applied for.

ISBN-13: 978-0-88150-703-4

Book design and composition by Hespenheide Design
Cover photo © 2006 James Kay
Interior photographs by the author unless otherwise indicated

Published by The Countryman Press, P.O. Box 748, Woodstock, VT 05091

Distributed by W. W. Norton & Company, Inc., 500 Fifth Avenue, New York, NY 10110

For my lovely wife, Tricia, and my darling girls, Elizabeth and Emma.

Acknowledgments

I need to begin by thanking Wilderness Systems for generously donating their Tsunami 140. This amazing boat allowed me to cover a variety of waters safely, comfortably, and quickly. It is the perfect companion to float Utah.

Also thanks are in order to Werner Paddles and Garmin for donating the tools of the trade for this book. My paddle and GPS were invaluable along the way, and I couldn't have done the book without them.

I also want to express my complete appreciation, devotion, and love to my lovely wife, Trish, and darling daughters, Elizabeth and Emma. Their support and enthusiasm really made writing this book a joy. Their patience and support as Dad went off on yet another paddle trip was inspiring.

Thanks are also in order for my in-laws, Al and Carolyn Barney, who watched my kids when I could not take them along on a trip or two. Their help and support throughout this lengthy summer was amazing.

Finally, I must convey special thanks to my good friend Greg Tanner who joined me on a number of paddle trips, took photographs, and basically helped ensure the book got finished. His companionship, enthusiasm, secretarial skills, and endurance were incredibly important.

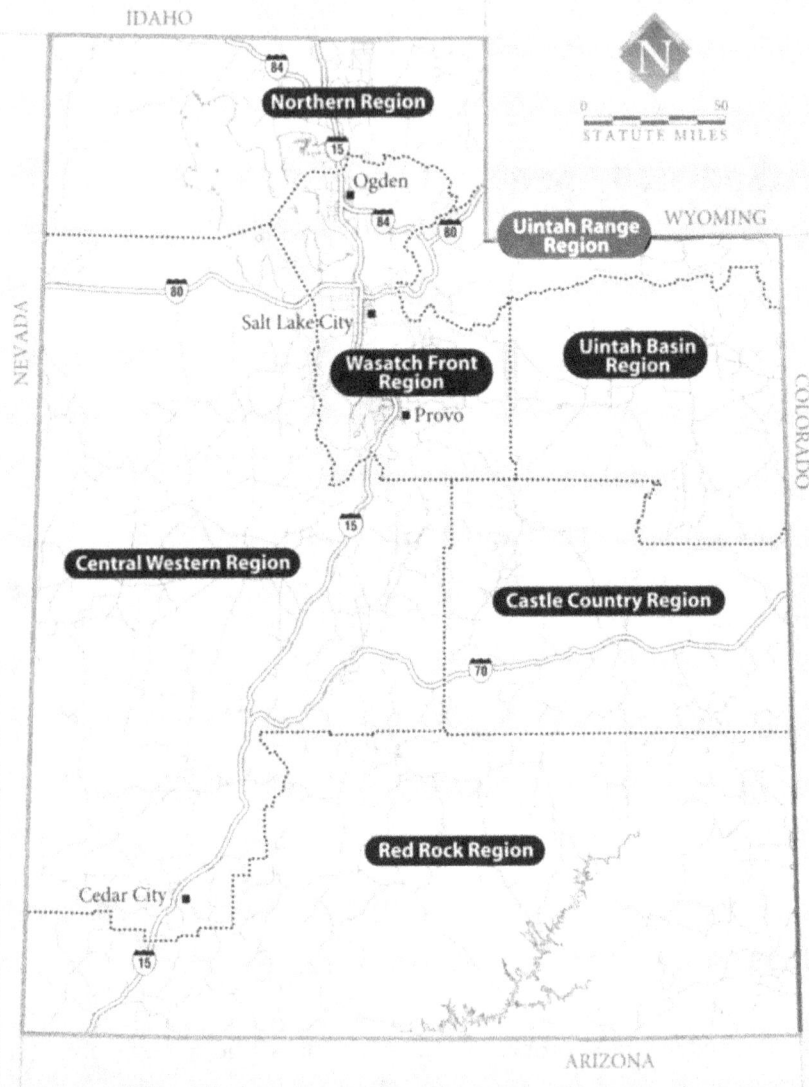

Contents

Introduction xiii

Part I: Practical Information
1. Paddling Tips 3
2. Destination Details 16

Part II: The Regions
3. Northern Region 33

Best Bets
    Bear Lake 35
    Tony Grove 37
    Porcupine Reservoir 40
    Mantua Reservoir 42
    Bear River Migratory Bird Refuge 45
    Cutler Marsh 48

Other Destinations
    Birch Creek Reservoir 51
    Cutler Reservoir 51
    Hyrum Reservoir 51
    Newton Reservoir 52
    Willard Bay 52
    Woodruff Creek Reservoir 53

4. Wasatch Front Region 55

Best Bets
    Great Salt Lake 58
    Pineview Reservoir 62
    Causey Reservoir 64
    Lost Creek Reservoir 67

Jordan River 69
Little Dell Reservoir 72
Weber River 75

Other Destinations

Currant Creek Reservoir 77
Deer Creek 78
East Canyon 78
Jordanelle Reservoir 78
Utah Lake 79
Soldier Creek and Strawberry Reservoir 79

5. Uintah Basin Region 81

Best Bets

Moon Lake 83
Lower Stillwater Ponds 86
Pelican Lake 89
Red Fleet Reservoir 91
Matt Warner Reservoir 93
East Park Reservoir 96

Other Destinations

Big Sand Wash 99
Boreham Lake (Midview Reservoir) 99
Bottle Hollow 100
Bullock Lake and Cottonwood Lake 100
Calder Reservoir 100
Crouse Reservoir 101
Starvation Reservoir 101
Steinaker Reservoir 102
Twin Pots 102

6. Uinta Range Region 103

Best Bets

Mirror Lake 108
Washington Lake 110
Spirit Lake 112
Browne Lake 114
Hoop Lake 116

Sheep Creek Lake 118
Smith and Morehouse Reservoir 121
Flaming Gorge Reservoir 123
Echo Reservoir 125

Other Destinations
Beaver Lake 127
Butterfly Lake 128
Lily Lake and Teapot Lake 128
Lily Lake #2 128
Lost Lake 129
Lyman Lake 129
Pass Lake 130
Rockport Reservoir 130
Trial Lake 130
Whitney Reservoir 131

7. Central Western Region 133

Best Bets
Mona Reservoir 136
Redmond Lake 138
Yuba Lake (Sevier Bridge Reservoir) 141
Johnson Valley Reservoir 143
Fish Lake 145
Forsyth Reservoir 148
Palisades Lake 150

Other Destinations
9 Mile 152
DMAD Reservoir (Delta Reservoir) 152
Gunnison Reservoir 154
Koosharem Reservoir 155
Mill Meadow 155
Minersville 155
Otter Creek Reservoir 156
Piute Reservoir 156
Rocky Ford Reservoir 157
Scipio Lake 157

8. **Castle Country Region 158**

Best Bets

    Millsite Reservoir 162
    Green River 164
    Joe's Valley Reservoir 167
    Boulger Lake, Electric Lake, CC Pond 169
    Cleveland Reservoir 172
    Huntington Reservoir (Mammoth Reservoir) 175

Other Destinations

    Huntington Lake 177
    Scofield Reservoir 177
    Miller Flat Reservoir 178

9. **Red Rock Region 179**

Best Bets

    Kolob Reservoir 183
    Lower Bowns Reservoir (Bowns Reservoir, Bounds Reservoir) 185
    Tropic Reservoir 187
    Pine Lake 189
    Lake Powell 192
    Navajo Lake 195
    Sand Hollow Reservoir 197
    Gunlock Reservoir 199

Other Destinations

    Ivins Reservoir 202
    Panguitch Lake 202
    Quail Creek Reservoir 202
    Recapture Lake 203
    Upper Enterprise Reservoir 203
    Wide Hollow Reservoir 204

Appendix 205

    Internet Resources 205
    Mileage Chart 206
    Government Resources 208
    Destinations by County 210
    Destination Elevations 214
    GPS Coordinates 218

Index 223

Introduction

There are few things I enjoy more than paddling. Sitting in the middle of a quiet lake breathes new life into me. In those moments, it is tranquil yet invigorating. The whole experience is the perfect tonic for my busy life.

I was inspired to assemble this book as I started to search for destinations to drag my canoe and kayaks to. Initially I simply cruised around the local reservoirs selecting destinations by convenience. My desire to experience other local waters turned me to my neighborhood bookstore. To my surprise, there was nothing there.

Paging through various guides about the state and reviewing titles on kayaking, I was stunned to discover while there were various regional books, nobody had written a paddling guide to Utah. In your hands, you hold my humble answer to this vacancy.

Paddling is wonderful in so many ways. It is a family activity that I can share with my wife and children. It is a great form of exercise. It is a chance for us to connect with nature and experience places that our feet can never take us. Last, it is an excuse to travel.

Over a summer, I visited more than one hundred different lakes, reservoirs, and rivers. I drove from border to border, nearly touching every corner of the state. I traveled more than 10,000 miles. The scenery was breathtaking, and the friendliness of people was constant. Every place I visited, people were supportive of my effort and provided helpful information.

Contained within these pages are locations in Utah that are unique, exciting, interesting, and in all, great places to paddle. While the book is meant to be comprehensive, some locations were excluded for a variety of different reasons—they were too isolated, too difficult, or just outright dull. I really focused on including destinations that are worth paddling.

Much of the material you will find in the front section of this book may seem familiar. However, it is actually tailored to your experience in paddling Utah. From the general state information and gear guide to the destination details, everything is focused on how to make the most of your flatwater paddle experience in this amazing place.

I have made Utah my home for the past 19 years because it has so much to offer my love of the outdoors. If you are just visiting, it is my wish that this book will help you make the most of your time here. If you are a resident, these pages contain destinations to discover on an errant weekend. Either way, I hope you find this book useful in your pursuit of similar pleasures.

THE BEEHIVE STATE

I consider myself fairly well traveled. I have made several trips to Europe. I have driven the United States from coast to coast. I have been lucky enough to visit some of the most beautiful and amazing destinations our world has to offer. And of all those places, many of them reside in the place I call home.

Utah is a beautiful and distinctive place. In writing this book, my travels carried me to every corner of the state. Every turn, every hill revealed a surprising and often picturesque location. From an idyllic pine-lined lake to a hidden desert oasis, my discoveries reveal that Utah's beauty is something to behold and enjoy.

The startling diversity of the landscape alone is a reason to make this state a vacation destination. Combine that with the abundant parks, kind people, and pleasant climate, and you have all the elements for a great vacation. However, paddling is not usually thought to be a reason for a visit.

Only 3.25 percent of the entire state of Utah is covered in water. It is an arid place with immense deserts and rugged mountains. The state contains a harsh landscape that is as diverse as it is scenic. It is world renowned for its skiing, national parks, camping, and biking. In all, Utah is an unsurpassed locale for incredible outdoor activities.

What is not widely known is that Utah is really a great place to paddle. Almost every spot to paddle in this state is surprising and interesting. Many I have discovered are an unexpected pleasure. As you scale mountain roads or trek desert highways, paddle locations simply appear. Utah is not a *typical* canoeing or kayaking experience.

Reservoirs, rivers, and lakes are located sporadically across the state. In some areas, there are abundant paddle choices. In others, you will find only one location within a hundred miles. Whether they are isolated or convenient, the destinations noted in this book will certainly be interesting.

In the following pages, you will find some new pleasures and some old friends. From world-renowned rivers to hidden mountain lakes, there is something for everyone looking for a flatwater paddle experience. It is my goal to provide you new excuses to get out on the water and to explore this fantastic state.

A DESERT DESIGNED

There is a place near Moab called Dead Horse Point. It is not a place to paddle. Rather, it is a location that overlooks a monstrous precipice created by millions of years of erosion. In a glance, you are reminded of the significant power of water. It can carve canyons, create communities, and make the most inhospitable place a home.

Throughout its history, Utah has had to deal with the limited water resources. Many of its cities and much of its history has developed around its rivers and lakes. The Native Americans and early fur traders established settlements in places where rivers met. The Mormon pioneers, who populated much of the state, designed systems of irrigation to accommodate their agrarian society.

In Utah, water is precious. Its lack of availability makes it the lifeblood that allows the state to survive and prosper. Many take for granted the water coming out of the faucet. Yet an importance must be placed on remembering that everyone in this state depends on a system of conservation, preservation, and protection.

CONSERVATION

It is critical to remember that water flows through Utah because it is managed. Our green landscapes, golf courses, and agriculture all depend on irrigation created through effective programs of water management. The distribution and ownership of water is significantly important to both the residents and businesses in the state.

Water management is part of the reality of living in Utah. One aspect of that management is the widespread presence of reservoirs. These constructed bodies of water contain the critical lifeblood needed for communities to survive during the dry months of summer. They are also major recreation destinations.

Each year as winter moves to spring, the warmth melts the mountain snow and the reservoirs capture the water. Depending on the location, the community, and of course, the amount of runoff, reservoirs can vary in size and function. The predominant form water storage takes in Utah is a reservoir.

Maintaining these locations as recreational destinations directly correlates to water use. The more you drink, water a lawn, wash a car, or take a shower, the less there is in the reservoir. Of course, each individual user can't consume these entire vast bodies. However, unbridled use by an entire population can place the state in a drought.

Conservation is the responsibility of everyone who lives in or visits Utah. From turning off the water while brushing your teeth to watering your lawn at night, every conservation measure ensures that we have water available for every purpose, especially paddling.

PRESERVATION

Coinciding directly with conservation, preservation of existing natural resources is of significant importance. Many people see a need to create new reservoirs to accommodate Utah's growing population. These proposals include damming existing rivers.

The problem with this scenario is that by creating new dams, we destroy existing habitats for wildlife. Many of the rivers and lakes that exist naturally will become threatened by the diversion of water. The passage of water from the mountains to the lakes and beyond is part of a larger ecosystem dependent on specific water flow.

With effective water management and conservation efforts, Utah will not need to create new dams. Even in years of drought, we have the ability to take responsibility for the water we use and be certain there is enough to go around.

It is our obligation to ensure that we are responsible with the water we use and protect the places it comes from. Creating new dams for the purposes of power or water is not a viable solution because it destroys other elements of our community. We need to maintain the areas we have and preserve the remaining natural areas for the future.

PROTECTION

The water you paddle is also the water you may be drinking. Thus, be conscientious and careful how you treat it. As all responsible campers know, it is important to *leave no trace*. The same holds true for responsible canoeists and kayakers.

It may be inconvenient to pack out your garbage or amusing to urinate into a lake, but the community that depends on the resource you are using is feeling the damage you are doing. Act responsibly and treat the water with the respect it deserves.

Utah's water is a critical resource that must be protected, preserved, and respected. Ever drop of water in this state is important to the population and wildlife. Our existence depends on residents and visitors taking protection into consideration.

More than 2 million acres of Utah are farmed. Combine that with more than 2 million residents, and the state has a significant demand for water. This resource is directly dependent on the normally abundant winter snowfall. Every year, as the snow covers our peaks, we know that will be what we drink the following season.

With a small effort by everyone, we can ensure that not only will we have abundant clean drinking water but also acres and acres of clean water to paddle. Pay respect to your community by protecting the water you use. Keeping our water clean is essential for everyone to benefit.

UTAH RIVERS COUNCIL AND PADDLE FESTIVAL

There is an organization in the state that works hard to ensure that the water we have is conserved, preserved, and protected. The Utah Rivers Council is a statewide, nonprofit organization that is focused on protecting Utah's rivers for future generations.

By providing education, information, and political resources, the council works for rivers and water of Utah. Its strong dedication to activism helps ensure our rivers remain wild, scenic. and untainted by human development.

This excellent organization sponsors a variety of events throughout the year to keep people aware of the importance of rivers in Utah. Paddling is an integral part of its mission. It uses the sport to help bring awareness to the issues surrounding rivers and to motivate activism.

The Utah Rivers Council's Paddle Festival is an annual event designed to expose people to the importance of protection and conservation while sharing the joys of paddling. The festival is unique in that it provides an opportunity for people to experiment with a variety of different boat styles. Local vendors and supporters of the council bring canoes and every variety of kayaks imaginable. In addition, local sailing enthusiasts will take you for a spin on a catamaran or sailboat.

Every year, participants can learn paddling skills through clinics. In addition to the learning opportunities, the event is also a great party with live music, terrific food, and activities for the kids. Plus, there is a large raffle where a ton of gear and a couple of boats are given away.

Everyone who values the paddling opportunities in this state should investigate the Utah Rivers Council. It is a great organization working to help keep Utah wild, natural, and scenic. Go to www.utahrivers.org.

CLIMATE

It is difficult, if not impossible, to describe Utah's climate in a single statement. Yet there is a common element among its regions. Utah is a dry place. From the mountainous north of the state to the red rocks of the south, most locations are arid.

This is not to say that Utah is absent of rain or moisture. In fact, its mountains receive more than 400 inches (10 meters) of snowfall annually. It rains and can be foggy and wet at times. However, humidity is rare, and Utah is mostly covered in desert.

With nine different climate zones, the state is a marvel of diversity and balance. While the high desert sees abundant snowfall and frequent rain, its dry base resists moisture. In fact, our world-renowned snow is a benefactor of the dry climate. It makes the white stuff powdery and light. Thus, the skiing in Utah is incredible. But that is the subject of another book.

SEASONS

Utah has beautiful seasons. You can find every flavor Mother Nature has to offer. Colorful autumns, bright hot summers, white winters, and lush springs are emblematic of the state. However, just because you can get all of these, that doesn't mean they are all in the same place.

Utah weather can vary depending on altitude and region. You can literally find completely different conditions within 15 minutes in some parts of the state. The harsh conditions of the mountains and desert are nothing to take lightly, and you need to understand what to expect during the different times of the year when you are planning a paddling trip.

SPRING

The spring season is a time of massive thaw. This means the lakes, rivers, and reservoirs are at their best and their most dangerous. Spring runoff contributes to most of the water the state drinks throughout the year. During this time, water rushes down from the mountains and fills up the dry areas of the state.

If you are paddling on a river in the spring, you can expect faster flow, larger rapids, and deeper channels. Lakes and reservoirs have easier portages and larger surface areas during this time as well. It is a great time to paddle.

Yet with more water comes the risk of flash floods and increased dangers. In addition, because the water is a product of melting snow, water temperatures are much cooler. It takes several weeks of sun to get the water warm enough for comfortably dipping in your feet.

Mountain lakes are still going to be inaccessible at this time of year, and until a good thaw is complete, you will not even be able to get to many of the popular destinations. Nonetheless, spring is a beautiful season in Utah. As everything around you awakens from its winter slumber, it is an excellent time to break out the paddle gear.

SUMMER

Summer is the season of paddling. It is an opportunity to explore areas normally buried by snow. The higher elevations experience summer rains and moisture with cool but pleasant temperatures. In fact, snow is not uncommon even in the heat of July. However, that is not a reflection of what you will experience in the remainder of the state.

I once saw a T-shirt that showed two skeletons sitting on the hood of an overheating jeep. Both appeared to be cooked alive. While smiling, one states, "Yeah, but it's a dry heat." This is what you can expect in most of Utah from July through early September.

Utah's summers are dry and hot. Temperatures can climb into the upper 90s or higher in almost every corner of the state. This is especially true in the southern portion, where you will find really scorching heat. However, there is little humidity. Thus, the burning hot sun is usually quite tolerable.

Add to this the fact that the state has a low elevation of about 2,000 feet (610 meters) and an average elevation around 6,200 feet (1,900 meters). You are closer to the sun here. Some areas of the state have harsh landscape, and the summer heat can be overwhelming. You must be properly prepared as you travel.

First, water is significantly important. You should always carry abundant amounts of it whenever traveling during the summer months. In the southern part of the state, keeping water in the vehicle is a year-round requirement. The simple fact is the temperatures are hot, and you can easily become dehydrated in Utah's dry climate.

Sunscreen is the next requirement. Utah elevations mean your skin is more susceptible to burning. The clear indigo skies are alluring and beautiful, but deceptively dangerous. No matter your skin type, generously applied sunscreen to exposed areas is a year-round necessity.

Last, eye protection is a must. As we all know, water reflects the sunlight. The glare and brightness of the Utah sun can cause long-term damage to eyes without proper protection. Whether you invest in an expensive pair or pick them up a local gas station, just make certain the glasses have 100 percent protection from ultra-violet (UV) rays.

AUTUMN

Few places are as beautiful as Utah in the autumn, and the state continues to provide paddling opportunities late into the year. Utah is blessed with Indian summers, which translates to warm days and cool nights, beautiful seasonal colors, and a longer-than-average paddling season.

In much of the state, you can paddle into early November. After that time, check your weather forecasts. If the snow has not covered the location, consider a dry suit or just head to the southern part of the state where the temperatures remain warm year-round.

Of course, the mountains experience cooler temperatures earlier, but I have paddled in October and November at the higher elevations on many occasions. As autumn dwindles into the winter, the temperatures dip into the freezing ranges. Once you start to see the mountains being covered with snow, it is time to consider putting up the paddle.

WINTER

For the most part, the state is cold or covered in snow. Only the southernmost locations can still be paddled. However, the water temperatures remain quite cool during the winter months and only the well-dressed and properly prepared venture forth onto the water during this season.

The only really realistic area you can paddle during the winter months will be the Red Rock region of the state. This area stays above freezing most of the winter, and in some cases, can have days with warm temperatures. However, the water will still be cold, and you will want to dress warmly if you venture out in your boat.

TRAVEL DATA

Utah is not exactly the easiest state to travel. With its vast distances and isolated communities, getting to the farthest regions requires a good vehicle and a patient temperament. Long stretches of vacant road are not uncommon. You will need to keep a full tank of gas and spry mind if you wish to safely traverse Utah's landscape.

The state has excellent roads, and for the most part, the destinations in this book do not require any special means of transportation. While a four-wheel-drive vehicle is definitely very useful if you plan on going off road, it is not really a requirement for those looking for a good paddle.

Three different interstate highways divide Utah. First, going from north to south, is I-15. This is the major route through the state, and it connects most of the state. The interstate runs from Canada to Mexico.

It is the major thoroughfare through Salt Lake and most other major cities in the state.

I-70 moves across the center of the state from Colorado to I-15. It connects much of the south to the rest of the state. Green River and Moab are the most known cities along the I-70 route. However, there are

You will need a full tank of gas to safely travel many areas of Utah.

many other towns in this area, and I-70 is used frequently by those traveling to the Red Rock region of the state.

The third major interstate is I-80. This road connects Utah to Wyoming and Nevada. It passes through Salt Lake and is a critical route to the High Uintas and the western desert. I-80 intersects with I-84 for a short jaunt through Morgan. However, I-84 reconnects to I-15 and heads north out of the state.

There are also two other key roads. US 89 and US 40 connect much of the state in the rural areas. US 40 connects the Uintah Basin to Salt Lake City. US 89 was the predecessor to I-15 and remains a major north-south connector.

With an understanding of these major routes, you will have an easier time establishing a quick path to many of the paddle destinations. The interstates provide a great method to get around the state, but a majority of your time will be spent on smaller roads.

DRIVING UTAH

Over the summer I wrote this book, I accumulated more than ten thousand miles of driving. On many occasions, I would travel a thousand miles in one weekend so I could reach the far corners of the state. There is a lot of open road in this state, and to get to a lot of the paddling destinations, you will need to spend hours on it.

A cell phone is a good idea in Utah, and coverage is fairly comprehensive. Of course, in the more remote spots, you are lucky to find even a radio signal. Yet even small towns have coverage, and there is consistent service on the interstates. You should check with your carrier to determine exactly where you will find coverage if you are venturing out.

There are places in Utah where you will go miles without any kind of service. You need to anticipate this prior to venturing into these primitive areas. Let people know when and where you are going before embarking on a paddle trip to these remote spots. Document your route and make a note of any details about where you are planning on staying.

In 2003, climber Aron Ralston was forced to cut off his arm after getting stuck while climbing in Utah's Canyonlands. He noted after the incident that had he left a note in his car or told people explicitly where he was climbing, search-and-rescue teams would have found him and possibly saved his arm.

By taking these simple precautions, you will ensure your safety in case something terrible happens. Paddling is not a dangerous activity, but unpredictable events can change that. With Utah's many isolated and remote areas, these kinds of details allow your friends and family to arrange a search in case something happens.

GRAVEL ROADS, ROCKS, AND RUTS

It is sad to admit, but there were lots of places I wanted to paddle that were just too difficult to reach. As I drove to some of the more remote corners of the state, I covered miles and miles of dirt and gravel roads. On one hand, there were places where the dirt roads were comparable to paved surfaces. On the other, there were more that had my hands shaking and my patience wearing thin.

Gravel and dirt roads are common in the mountains and rural parts of the state. Many places are accessible only a few months a year, and as such, there is no reason to spend valued tax dollars improving roads that get so little use. Thus, it is important to note a few things before you decide to make a trip to one of the bodies of water that is accessible by dirt or gravel roads.

First, roads can change condition. Depending on the weather, the surface of a dirt road can go from smooth to treacherous. Before you choose a route, it might make sense to check with the local ranger or park service office to ensure the roads are accessible.

Next, you may want to consider the clearance of your vehicle. Traditional autos do not have a lot of room between the ground and the underside of the car. This means rocks and gravel can create damage if you are not careful. You will want to observe posted speed limits and watch the road for rocks, branches, snow, etc.

Last, Utah is a mountainous state. You will find areas with steep descents and climbs. On the way up these hills, your engine may warm up. You should look to see if your coolant and oil are filled. On the way down, your brakes are critical. Be certain you have them checked if you know you will be taking on this kind of terrain.

In all, much of the state is very easy to drive. You will find few serious road conditions to contend with when you go on a paddle trip. However, a car is part of your survival gear in the rural regions of the state. Being unprepared can leave you isolated and in danger.

THE CATTLE GUARD

Across the rural landscape of Utah, cattle are common. You see cows everywhere you go. However, cows do not observe the rights-of-way. Many times as I crossed the state, I had to slow down to wait for "Bessie" to cross. If you see cattle, slow down and watch their movement. A little patience is important if you do not want a side of beef on your vehicle.

Ranchers attempt to prevent their livestock from wandering beyond the confines of their ranch with simple things like fences. However, Utah has a lot of open range, and a common tool to keep the cows off the road is called a cattle guard.

The cattle guard is a series of pipes embedded across a section of road. Imagine a small bridge made of pipe. For some reason, cattle are very sensitive to their stability, and these guards frighten them. The cows will not attempt to cross the cattle guard, and thus, they are kept in a confined ranch area.

Cattle guards are common fixtures on Utah roads and can be disconcerting. First, they can startle you while driving. The loud rumble as you cross may shock you if you are driving at night. Next, the road can narrow at a guard location. Last, guards are not always well maintained and can be rough to cross.

These two do not know the traffic laws.

Cattle are known to roam. Their stomachs drive their direction, and they will wander aimlessly looking for another bite of fresh grass. Being careful in cattle country will ensure your safety as you trek to some of the more remote paddle destinations.

ODDITIES AND ODYSSEYS

Utah is a unique place in many ways. Besides its scenery, the history, people, and culture are distinctively different than the rest of the United States. By the same token, it is a very *American* place with a strong sense of patriotism and common elements that you will find across the country.

Understanding these differences will help you in your travels around the state and allow you enjoy all it has to offer. The following information explains some of the local idiosyncrasies and issues and how to deal with them.

THE MORMONS, BEER, AND A GOOD CUP OF COFFEE

Over the years as I have traveled, whenever I note that I am from Utah, the inevitable question arises, "Are you a Mormon?" While I am not of that faith, it is true that Utah is the proverbial Rome for the Mormons, and they represent a majority of the population of the state. This is a good thing.

Mormons are clean-living, friendly, and amicable people. Most are very devout, and all have a strong sense of family and community. Part of their core belief system is to seek new members. Young men and women are sent around the world to spread their message. Thus, as you travel the state of Utah, you will usually find a friendly face and a warm greeting waiting for you.

The Mormon church is much more dominant in the smaller communities than around Salt Lake City. However, it is present everywhere. That is not to imply that other faiths are obscure. In fact, if you are visiting from out of town, it is very likely you will find your particular faith represented in every corner of the state.

Many know the Mormons are teetotalers and mistakenly think that it is impossible to purchase alcohol in the state. In fact, it is quite the contrary. Alcohol is easily obtainable; while there are a couple of strange rules, you can buy alcohol seven days a week (yes, even on Sunday) in a restaurant or bar.

You can purchase beer in convenience stores and grocery stores every day. Hard liquor can be purchased from state-owned stores from 10 AM to 10 PM every day but Sunday. Brewpubs are scattered across the state, and many produce award-winning beers. In addition, most of the ones I have visited have terrific food and wonderful service.

Mormons also abstain from beverages containing caffeine, yet coffee shops are easy to locate. Whether you want a local brew or you are nursing an addiction to Starbucks, you can find that four-dollar cup of coffee whenever you need it.

In all, the Mormons are a positive influence on the state. They settled the region more than 150 years ago and set up irrigation in a barren desert. We owe many of the paddle destinations in this book to their ingenious methods of conservation and foresight for population growth.

SUNDAY, SUNDAY

Yes, many things close on Sunday in Utah. In fact, in some of the smaller towns, you may find that everything is closed and the town is basically shut down. This can be an issue if you are looking to buy gas or food. Traveling to the outer reaches of the state means you will need effective planning.

The Mormon population has a strong credo that Sunday is a special day and that work is frowned upon. This means members will close their places of business and attend church. While service stations, hospitals, and other necessities are typically open, restaurants, grocery stores, and many other businesses close on Sunday.

Sunday closings in the larger metropolitan areas are not as significant an issue. However, if you notice you need gas in one of the very remote areas of the state, you will not want to tempt fate or be cheap about gas prices when you see an open business.

NATIVE AMERICAN NATIONS

Utah has literally thousands of acres of Native American reservations, and the tribes are considered nations. They have some paddle locations on their lands, and they usually welcome use. However, their property is not bound by the same laws and rules as the rest of the state. Sometimes they will require a special permit or exclude use entirely.

I have noted waters in this book that are on tribal lands and the rules governing their use. Yet there may be some I missed, and if you see a sign posted indicating the property is owned by a particular tribe, you will want to contact them before using it. As with any place you might visit, observe all posted signs and respect the rules.

FEES AND PERMITS

There are many paddle destinations noted in this book that require fees for their use. I had planned to include fee information, but then realized that these change from year to year and sometimes from location to location. Thus, the information I would be providing would become useless fairly quickly.

You can anticipate that most major parks, both state and national, will charge fees for their use. In some cases, you will find use fees at the county and local level, but that is far less common. In addition, administration of fees depends on administration and management of a site.

The fees are usually not excessive, and you should check out what they are before traveling. I have seen costs ranging from a couple of dollars to as much as ten. Of course, the more time you spend at the site, the more you will have to pay.

Utah currently does not require a permit on anything that does not have an engine. However, if you slap a little trolling motor on your canoe, you may need a boat permit. Check with the state government on

The Uintahs are the ceiling of Utah and have elevations up to thirteen thousand feet.

the current laws regarding permits because the fines for not complying can be severe.

I found very few fees while I was out paddling, and most reservoirs are open for public use at no charge. Yet if you have to pay a fee, don't feel bad. The money gathered is usually to help maintain the area you are using. This small price compensates for the enjoyment you will experience paddling.

UINTAH VERSUS UINTA

When Fred Astaire sang "Let's Call the Whole Thing Off" in *Shall We Dance*, he was arguing the merits of keeping a relationship alive when there were so many inherent differences in how he and Ginger Rogers spoke. As I tried to find an accurate spelling of Uintah versus Uinta, I almost called off writing about the region.

The simple fact is I can't find any conclusive evidence that supports either spelling. At times, they seem interchangeable and then some official documentation demands one of the versions. Like watching a virtual tennis match, the letter *h* appears and disappears as often as you shift your eye through text.

To make matters worse, the pronunciation of both is virtually identical. It would be nice if someone emphasized the *ah* sound or used brevity when speaking the *uh*. The two spellings are synonymous and the differences indiscernible when spoken by a Utah native.

So let me point out the merits of both sides of the argument. First, we have the Uintah Basin. This includes Uintah County and a local paper that clearly uses the *h* in its publications. Throughout this region of central eastern Utah, you know that this spelling is appropriate.

However, enter our friends from Uinta National Forest. The U.S. federal government has tossed off the *h* for this massive region of the state. This large area of forested land contains a huge concentration of mountain lakes, and thus, I am inclined to support the absence of the letter.

In the end, the argument is unclear. I concluded that I would go with the locals.

I will make an honest effort to be consistent in this book. If you see the letter *h* attached to your Uinta, then you can assume that I found some reference to the spelling in my research. In contrast, if you have lost your letter *h* on a Uintah, please don't fret. It might simply be a case of me being lazy.

Practical Information

PART I

Utah paddling is unique, exciting, and interesting.

Paddling Tips

Water is an interesting thing. Its fluidity means it is constantly changing. It is our lifeblood, while at the same time, one of the most destructive forces in the world. It also has amazing variety. The ocean is nothing like a lake, which is nothing like a river, which is nothing like any other form water takes. Water can be broken down to two parts hydrogen and one part oxygen. Yet its characteristics can be different in so many ways.

Utah's waters are unique, and thus, this portion of the book is focused on making certain you are properly equipped for your excursions around the state. This book is exclusively focused on slow-moving rivers and flatwater lakes and reservoirs. The gear described is not for whitewater kayaking, river rafting, or any other form of boating. It is only for canoes and kayaks that want to float calm waters.

As a paddler, you may already have most of the gear noted in this chapter. Or there may be some items you need to add to your equipment. If you are embarking upon paddling as a hobby, the information will provide you a comprehensive list of the items you should have to ensure a safe and enjoyable time on the water.

PERSONAL FLOTATION DEVICE (PFD) OR LIFE JACKET

It is no accident that a personal flotation device (PFD) or life jacket is the first article of gear being covered. Quite simply, it is the most important. You should never enter the water in a canoe or kayak without one. Even the calmest water can become deadly if you paddle without a PFD.

Statistics show that 75 percent of all people who drowned in boating accidents might have survived if they wore a PFD. This is a sobering number considering a life jacket is fairly inexpensive, convenient, and if properly selected, comfortable.

You can find a variety of shapes and styles of life jackets. No matter which one you choose, the PFD must be U.S. Coast Guard (USCG) certified. There are five types of ratings for these jackets. Each classification has a different purpose. The only one of the five you need to be concerned about is the Type III.

The Type III PFD is perfect for paddling. In an accident, the jacket design forces the wearer into a face-up position in the water. While it will provide flotation for as long as necessary, the jacket is really focused on situations where you will be rescued quickly.

You can identify these jackets by the USCG Type III certification imprinted on the interior of the jacket. In most cases, a small booklet accompanies the jacket with instructions for correct fitting and use of the PFD. You will find that this variety of PFD is easy to locate and is perfect for Utah's waters.

If your own safety is not a satisfactory motivation, Utah state law requires that you wear a PFD. On lakes, a jacket is required in boats over 16 feet long. On rivers, the law states that everyone on a boat must wear a properly fitted U.S. Coast Guard-approved PFD. So there are few instances where a jacket can be removed.

Regardless, nobody can predict when an accident will happen. You might be alone on a lake without another soul in sight, and the weather could suddenly change. You could roll or fall out. You could have a medical emergency. The simple fact is that your life is more important than any issues you might have with comfort or convenience. Invest in a quality PFD, and you will enjoy your boat for years to come.

SELECTING A PFD

PFDs for paddling have improved over the years. Many manufacturers design vests with large armholes to offer easier paddling movement. In addition, the vests have multiple straps to get the perfect fit. Some provide convenient pockets and hooks for your gear. Of course, as you add additional features, you add cost. Whatever jacket you choose, it is important to remember a few key things.

First, make certain the PFD fits properly. It should be comfortable and close-fitting. You do not want the vest to be too loose or too tight. If it is too loose, it could float over your head. If it is too tight, it can cause difficulty breathing and will be generally uncomfortable. When fitting the jacket, the adjustable straps are often in awkward places. Enlist the help of a friend to ensure you get it just right.

Next, depending on your boat, you may want to look at where the PFD sits in relation to your waist and seat. In kayaks with small cockpits, you may want to have a higher cut jacket. However, a full-sized PFD might work nicely for your canoe. There are jackets specifically designed for the different flavors of paddling. You ought to try on a few before making your purchase.

Finally, the last factor to consider is jacket color. While many styles and designs are available, you might consider one that is bright and easy to see. Of course, color preference is a big part of any decision. However, jacket color has real importance. It is possible that you could end up in the water. A bright color will help you stand out against the water and will help search-and-rescue personnel if you need their assistance.

OTHER SAFETY ESSENTIALS

Beyond the PFD, there are several other items that help prevent accidents and make your boating experience safer. Each of the following items should be considered standard equipment for paddling. Moreover, you may want to build yourself a small pack where you can place these essentials.

WHISTLE

It is amazing how sound travels. I can be sitting in a movie theater with the latest sound system blaring and still manage to hear that guy three rows up unwrapping his candy. A whistle works on the same premise. Its high pitch and excellent volume can draw attention of people who are quite a distance away. It is also an effective device for scaring away wildlife and notifying other boaters of your presence.

There are whistles specifically designed for camping and paddling, but any whistle will do. I suggest finding one with a nice clip so you can attach it to your PFD. In addition, you may want to avoid metal versions because they can rust. An inexpensive plastic whistle does the job perfectly. Add a floating keychain to carry it on, and you are set.

THROW ROPE

A throw rope is essentially a rope in a bag. The key in its design is that it is compact and can be hurled across the water. When used correctly, the bag becomes a quick and effective way to reach out to a paddler in need. Simply grab one end and toss the other into the water. The throw rope is a lifeline in times of danger.

These compact little bags are a convenient and important safety tool for paddlers. They are mostly used on rivers in situations where a paddler becomes swamped. However, they are just as useful in rough water or in cases where someone simply needs your help. They are an excellent and necessary investment that could save a life.

ROPE

Unlike a throw rope, this is simply a utilitarian accessory designed to simplify tasks while out on the water. It should be carried in addition to a throw rope. The throw rope usually never leaves the bag unless it is an emergency. However, your rope will see regular use.

A length of rope is a useful companion. From tying up an errant canoe to towing a tired paddling partner, rope has innumerable uses and takes up very little space. Keep about 15 feet of a good quality woven material. I prefer climbing rope because it comes in a variety of colors and is very strong.

You should also consider a bright color because it better defines a towline, which could be used to help flag someone down in an emergency situation. In addition, consider stowing the rope in a convenient location so you can access it easily.

POCKETKNIFE

I carry a Swiss Army knife with me everywhere. Every day, this friendly little tool finds some use. Whether it is opening letters at the office or stripping a wire at home, this knife is a constant companion. On the water, it even finds more use from fixing a broken boat to cutting a length of rope. I feel I need my knife to ensure I am prepared for any situation.

Like life, paddling is unpredictable, and a pocketknife remains a useful tool that everyone should carry. Whether you prefer a Leatherman, Swiss Army knife, or straight blade, keep your trusty knife accessible—in a convenient pocket, attached to a key chain, or connected to your PFD.

FIRST-AID KIT

Paddling is a relatively safe sport. However, anyone who spends time on the water knows that cuts and bruises are common. If you throw fishing into the mix, the chances of a cut triple. The point is a small first-aid kit is a useful and necessary companion to anyone who plans on paddling.

There are numerous packaged kits out there that do the job nicely. However, it is easy to build one at home, and it can be less expensive. The following are medical items to consider including in your kit:

Tweezers
Waterproof matches
Band-Aids of varying sizes
Purell or other brand of hand sanitizer
   (*for cleaning hands only*)
Alcohol prep pads
   (*for cleaning wounds*)
Antibiotic ointment
   (*Neosporin*)
Pain reliever
   (*ibuprofen, aspirin, etc.*)
Scissors
Medical adhesive tape
Gauze pads
Latex gloves
First-aid guide

Place all these materials in a small, clear, dry box or bag. When emergencies arrive, it is essential to be able to quickly locate a particular item. Having a clear container makes it a lot easier to find things. Always do a quick inventory before each trip.

In addition to the items noted, you may want to include personal items that are particular to your medical or physical condition. For example, I always pack some allergy medicine in case the pollen count gets too high. While this may seem a touch cautious, you never know when a short day on the lake can go longer than you expect.

WATER AND FOOD

Most of the emphasis of this book is concerned with the kind of water you float on; however, the water you drink is of greater importance. Kayaking and canoeing are athletic endeavors and require sufficient hydration. Water is a critical aspect of any activity, and your safety and survival depends on you keeping hydrated.

Keep in mind, water is not simply a thirst quencher. It is used to keep your body cool through perspiration. As you paddle, you are perspiring and losing fluids. The more you exercise the more water you have to consume. The best way to avoid dehydration is to keep about a liter of water on hand. Slowly sipping it while exercising replenishes your lost fluids.

In addition, many of the locations in this book lack any close services for items like food and water. You should be properly prepared with an adequate supply of snacks and beverages before taking a paddle excursion. Whatever your taste, your body needs fuel to operate. Paddling is a much more enjoyable sport when you are comfortable.

ESSENTIAL PADDLING GEAR

BOATS

Considering the variety of canoes and kayaks available for purchase, a novice might be worried. However, one of the great things about paddling flat water is that if something floats, you pretty much can paddle it. This isn't to say that different boat styles won't perform better or worse. It simply means that you can use almost any kind of boat on the waters described in this book.

I will not go into the details of the different kinds of boats or the abundant features and forms that are available. There are far better resources to help in this effort. However, I will note a few important things that you may want to consider when investing in either a kayak or canoe.

First, because the focus of this book is on flatwater paddling, you may want to consider the hull design. A boat that has either a very small keel or V-shaped hull provides excellent paddling efficiency. These features help ensure the boat maintains a straight path in the water with less paddling effort. However, a keel somewhat reduces maneuverability.

A flat-bottom boat is much more stable on calm water. On lakes or slow-moving rivers, the paddling can get a little tiresome if you have to continually straighten your course. Conversely, you can stand up in a flat-bottom boat if you want to fish.

Next, you may want a boat that provides storage. There are numerous small items that you should bring along on every trip. A canoe has an open design, and storage holds are not normally an option. However, kayaks normally have these places, and I use mine often.

Another thing to consider is the seating. If you have an uncomfortable seat, no matter how nice the scenery might be, you are not going to enjoy your paddling. Be certain to test it out before investing in a boat. Aftermarket seats for kayaks and canoes are available if you already own a boat.

Last, be certain to invest in something lightweight and durable. You will find your boat sitting in the garage a lot if it is a struggle to carry or if you put a hole in it. Even the most cautious paddlers will scratch and bump their boat. Investing in these aspects will ensure long use and enjoyment.

There are other factors like size, shape, and style to investigate. You will find excellent resources on canoe and kayak manufacturers' Web sites to help steer you in the direction of a boat that suits your needs. Companies like Wilderness, Dagger, Old Town, Mad River, and others have buying guides and customer-service lines to help as well.

PADDLES

Your paddle is both your motor and your steering wheel. This is what propels you and guides you through the water. As with boats, there are innumerable combinations of blade design and shaft materials for both canoes and kayaks. There are five prominent features to consider—blade shape, construction, durability, weight, and length. Excellent paddles are lightweight and strong and have blades that are efficient and productive for paddling. Of course, the top of the line can cost as much as a boat.

Canoe paddles are typically wood and crafted by hand. Kayak paddles are typically made with synthetic materials, because you need to separate the components for storage or twist them for different paddling angles. Just like with boats, I will defer to other experts on selecting an appropriate paddle for your use. Paddle makers like Werner, Bending Branches, and Carlisle are a few who can help guide you to right the paddle.

GPS RECEIVER

Technology enhances our life in many ways. While paddling is normally a reprieve from technology, one tool represents significant value and should be considered a must-have accessory for paddling. This is a GPS.

GPS stands for global positioning system; more accurately, the tool is called a receiver. The receiver provides a means to determine latitude and longitude using signals from a network of satellites. Through triangulation, this handy little device pinpoints your location and derives a lot of valuable information.

On a superficial level, it can tell you your speed, altitude, and direction. By adding maps, the detail even gets more relevant. A GPS receiver can track your route, estimate times of arrival, measure distances, and even provide ideal routes to get you to your destination.

I own a Garmin 76CS and use it to get back to my put-in, measure the distance I have paddled, and note places I visit so I can return to them later. Even more valuable, it is an excellent tool to help determine my time on the water and how long before I will get to a camp spot.

In my effort to get all the data for this book, I set marks called waypoints that provided me with altitude, coordinates, and a quick way to find the locations on the map. I found multiple other uses for my GPS while paddling, including measuring distances to locations and providing information about sunrise and sunset.

The GPS is a useful tool and can also be an important safety accessory. The device has a breadcrumb function that will actually show your track. It is hard to get lost when you know exactly where you are and where you have been and have access to maps showing you where you are going.

BILGE PUMP AND SPONGE

It is inevitable that if you are in a boat, you are going to get water in said boat. The simple fact is canoes and kayaks are wet vehicles, and you are not likely to stay dry for any extended period of time. Whether it is chop on the water, splashes from your fellow paddlers, or simply a tip in the wrong direction, water is going to get in your boat. In these cases, there are two tools that will help.

The first and most useful is the hand bilge pump. Placing the end into the water at the bottom of your boat, the small hand pump swallows up the water and spits it over the side. Even a boat with several inches of water can be emptied relatively quickly using a bilge.

The second tool is for those spots that you can't reach with the pump. A bilge sponge absorbs water in hard-to-reach spots and in places where the hand pump would be ineffective. Most people invest in the pump and forego a sponge, but for paddlers who need all the water out, the bilge sponge is an efficient tool.

Last, those who border on obsessive when it comes to a dry boat could invest in a deck towel. Similar to those you buy to dry your car, a deck towel is an exceptionally absorbent piece of cloth designed to remove water from the items in your boat. It isn't going to empty a boat filled with water, but it works nicely when clearing a dry space for your camera or GPS.

DRY BAGS

It only takes one spill into a lake to remind you of the importance of a dry bag. Normally soft-sided and easy to pack, a dry bag is airtight and protects your gear from the water.

Typical dry bags have a rolled top that locks out the water while capturing air on the inside. The true test of a quality dry bag is to fill it with air and then close the bag. If no air escapes, you can be assured that your gear will remain safe and dry. Cheap dry bags leak air, and that means water is inevitably going to leak into the bag.

If you are not one for camping from your canoe or kayak, you should still invest in a small bag for items like your wallet, cell phone, and car keys. Be certain to keep it attached to your boat with a length of rope, and be sure the bag has a lot of air in it. This way if you swamp, the bag and your essentials will float.

Dry boxes are airtight containers but have hard sides and are less maneuverable to store in a boat. However, they can't be crushed, and they protect items like cameras and electronics more effectively.

PORTAGE

While many of the waters noted in this book are very well accommodated, you may find a few occasions where a portage will be required. I have tried to note where boat ramps are located or simple beach entry is possible. Depending on the destination, you may want to drive around and do some exploration to find a spot.

Factors like the number of people in your party, your gear, and the duration of your trip dictate what spot is the best portage for you. I have been known to haul my stuff a couple hundred yards because I am too eager to paddle. Often a short scouting expedition will reveal an ideal location for you and your boat.

If you spend a lot of time on the water, small carts are available that allow you to easily haul your boat to the water. This saves multiple trips between the car and the boat. Some of these carts actually tear down, and you can simply toss them in the boat.

SUNGLASSES, SUNSCREEN, AND HAT

Utah sits at high elevations, and as such, you should consider taking proper protection from the sun. Investing in a good pair of sunglasses, a bottle of sunscreen, and a hat will help shield you from the harmful UV rays and prevent sunburn.

The glare from the water can cause permanent eye damage. Invest in a pair of sunglasses with 100 percent UV protection. In addition, you may want to consider polarized glasses. These reduce the reflective glare and provide the added benefit of better clarity when on the water.

Sunscreen comes in a variety of flavors and provides protection based upon an SPF rating. The higher the rating, the more protection provided. SPF 30 is very effective for paddling and should be applied on all exposed areas. However, depending on your skin type, you may need more or less protection.

Last I always wear a hat when I paddle. It not only provides excellent sun protection, but it is also an effective tool for cooling your body in the heat. A hat acts as a venting system by absorbing perspiration.

JACKET

In the mountains, the climate can change suddenly. The tall peaks hide pending weather patterns, and what starts out as a good day can turn terrible very quickly. If you happen to get rained on or get too wet during a paddle trip, a jacket can help prevent a serious situation.

Hypothermia is caused by the combination of wind, wet, and cold. The wind creates a chill in the body, the water absorbs your body heat, and the cold induces the hypothermia. Paddling can deliver all three of these very easily, and a good jacket can prevent it very effectively.

I suggest packing something lightweight and compact that will prevent you from getting saturated by rain. Where and when you are paddling should dictate the type of coat you tote along. Be certain to pack it in a dry bag so that it doesn't get wet.

BUG SPRAY

Where there is water, there are bugs. Mosquitoes, gnats, flies, and other pesky insects are invited to a veritable feast when you decide to go out for a paddle. As such, a good-quality bug spray is a necessary accessory.

Recent years have complicated the whole bug-spray scene. In the past you had the choice of pine and pine. Now you can get your bug spray in multiple aromatic scents with sunscreen and without harmful chemicals. Personally, I still like the pine scent, but people's chemistries differ, and one of these new scents or formulas may be better suited to you.

CHECKLIST

Here is a handy checklist of items that you should consider bringing on every trip regardless of its duration:

- ❏ PFD
- ❏ Boat
- ❏ Paddle
- ❏ Bilge pump
- ❏ Sponge
- ❏ Deck towel
- ❏ Throw rope
- ❏ Rope
- ❏ First-aid kit
- ❏ Whistle
- ❏ Pocketknife
- ❏ Sunglasses
- ❏ Sunscreen
- ❏ Hat
- ❏ Bug spray
- ❏ Water
- ❏ Food
- ❏ GPS
- ❏ Camera
- ❏ Jacket

CHAPTER 2

Utah is about contrast, and the paddle destinations will give you a taste of all the state has to offer.

Destination Details

This is both a travel book and a paddle guide. My effort has been concentrated on collecting details about various locations to paddle throughout the state of Utah. While this book attempts to be comprehensive, it is simply impossible to paddle every single body of water. There are numerous areas that are inaccessible by anything other than hiking. Some locations are dry during most of the year. Others are just not worth paddling.

The destinations noted in the book have a number of elements in common. First, most are relatively easy to access. Next, they are worthy places to paddle. They provide a good experience for someone looking for some flat water to float. Last and most obvious, all of these places are in Utah.

Within this section, you can obtain guidance on reviewing the destinations included in this book. With each of the "Best Bets," I have included a number of specific details that will help make your visit safe and enjoyable. Essentially, you will find the details about the details.

It is important to remember that there is always another perspective to consider. Your surroundings, experience, and upbringing impact your view of the world. Thus, it is important to note that the material provided is written in the context of my experiences in the state of Utah.

You may not consider some of the large bodies of water to be large. Some of the smaller bodies of water might not seem worth paddling. But it is simply a matter of perspective. I have tried to provide reasons that justify why I selected a particular body of water to be included.

My goal in writing this book is to give a taste of each location while providing factual, informative, and hopefully entertaining details. It is not my intention to simply categorize the waters of the state of Utah. Rather, I hope that reading this book will encourage you to pull the boat out of the garage and trek to some of these spectacular locations.

REGIONAL INFORMATION

The book has broken the state into seven regions. The areas within a region are associated with one another because of a common geography and geology. These seven regions are also grouped together by county. Each of the counties in the region intersects with another in some form.

The following is a list of the regions, a brief description of each region, and the counties it contains:

CASTLE COUNTRY REGION

High plateaus and unique mountain terrain, the Castle Country Region is geologically diverse and centrally located.
Counties: Carbon, Emery, Grand

CENTRAL WESTERN REGION

Isolated and massive, this region has many paddling jewels hidden among the acres and acres of open terrain.
Counties: Iron, Beaver, Millard, Juab, Tooele, Sanpete, Sevier

NORTHERN REGION

Characterized by lush farmlands and towering mountains, the Northern Region is a green area with early winters and beautiful summers.
Counties: Box Elder, Cache, Rich

RED ROCK REGION

Famous for its national parks and stunning scenery, the Red Rock Region has unique paddle destinations in amazing locations.
Counties: Washington, Kane, Piute, San Juan, Garfield

UINTAH BASIN REGION

Home to remnants of dinosaurs and to the foothills of the Uinta Range, this region is a study in diverse contrasts. Mountains and desert are just a short distance from one another.
Counties: Duchesne, Uintah

UINTA RANGE REGION

Utah's high country, the Uinta Range is characterized by towering mountains and amazing alpine lakes.
Counties: Summit, Daggett, Duchesne

WASATCH FRONT REGION

The urban center of the state, this region is about convenient paddling near the metropolitan areas.
Counties: Weber, Davis, Utah, Morgan, Salt Lake, Wasatch

While it might be hard to believe, there is more to life than paddling. Every regional section provides interesting aspects about the area and surrounding attractions. I have emphasized some of the major cities and tried not to overlook anyone. However, the selected listings were based on services available for paddlers.

My notations are casual, and I encourage anyone visiting these regions to explore the other activities available. In the more rural areas, I emphasize the parks and natural sites that are distinct to the region. In the cities, I note events, architecture, and activities. My goal is to help you make the most of your visit to the area.

There is simply not enough space to give you all the details and still make this book about paddling. The Internet provides excellent information about the abundant sites and activities in the state. My hope is that these regional sections will bring to light a few that you may not have considered.

BEST BETS

The rest of this chapter details the elements included with each of the Best Bets. Whenever possible, the most accurate information has been provided. However, there may be instances where you might want to gather more data before your visit. For example, weather, conditions, or rules are topics that can't be covered in the scope of this book, but could have a bearing on your paddle adventure.

Please remember that things change; while I have attempted to be both meticulous and as comprehensive as possible, you may still need a touch more data. Every paddler needs to be responsible and properly prepare for his or her time on the water.

NAME

The name provided is how the body of water is commonly identified on maps and in GPS software. In every case, the book will provide the most accurate name possible. Of course, many areas have different names, nicknames, and prior names. If there are multiple names for a body of water, it will be noted at the top, but not in the text of the destination's description.

In addition, there are multiple locations with duplicate names. In those cases, I have either identified the general location of the water or provided a clear landmark that will allow you to immediately discern which lake I am referencing. It is best to correlate the name with the county or location so you can ensure that you have accurate information.

COUNTY

Utah is broken into 29 different counties. In each region of the book, there is a map of the area that includes the county names and locations. Each destination includes its county.

County borders are not simple geometric patterns. They take on varying shapes and forms and can cover different terrain. Not every border is clearly identifiable, and some places may not be accessible from one county into another. The county system is an effective method for quickly locating something on a state map, but it may not be the quickest route to the destination.

Some of the water noted in this book is managed by its respective county, and thus, rules and fees can vary. County-managed property usually does not differ from the state-run facilities. However, state and federal park passes are not usually accepted for access.

LONGITUDE/LATITUDE

There are a number of methods for locating the paddle destinations noted in this book. The maps or directions are adequate. In fact, you could even use the county guide to assist in your search. However, the ideal method would be to plot the location on a map or GPS unit using the longitude and latitude.

Using these two numbers, you can plot any location on the globe. The system was invented so that a ship's captain could specify a location on a map without the need of landmarks. He or she could simply identify specific coordinates and plot them on a map.

Longitude runs north to south from pole to pole and is also referred to as meridian. Latitude runs east to west covering the circumference of the globe in varying lengths. (The longest latitude is the equator, which bisects earth.) Both are divided at varying distances depending where you are on the planet.

The lines are evenly distributed around the globe and are provided in measurements of degrees, minutes, and seconds. These numbers are easy to use with a GPS or a well-defined map. Simply entering the coordinates noted in the book should help you quickly and efficiently locate the paddle location.

Yet it is important to note that the longitude and latitude coordinates provided are not exact. They are intended to be used solely for directional purposes. GPS devices vary in accuracy, and some are accurate to within only 100 meters. Thus, do not use them to plot exact locations.

The latitude and longitude provided will help you track the locations noted in the book. However, water levels change from year to year, as does the Utah landscape. These coordinates are simply a method to help identify where a body of water is located.

ELEVATION

In this book, you will find paddling destinations as high as 10,000 feet, and a third of the paddles are over 8,000. There is a direct correlation between the elevations and the seasons of Utah. Many of the most beautiful spots to paddle exist at elevations that prohibit access until the summer months. In fact, snowfall is not unheard of at the higher elevations even in midsummer.

In addition, travelers to Utah will need to note the elevation and take into consideration altitude sickness. There is definitely a difference between sea level and 10,000 feet. The thin air can cause headaches, nausea, and dizziness. It is a serious condition, and often people need to acclimate themselves before ascending to higher elevations.

BODY TYPE

When describing a body of water, it is common to refer to it by its technical name. However, those names mean different things to different people. What you might call a lake, someone else might refer to as a pond. A stream could be a small river, while a tributary could be a large stream. The following three descriptions are used in this book:

Reservoir

The vast majority of the waters noted in this book are reservoirs. These constructed bodies of water are designed to provide water storage during the dry seasons of the year. Most are tied to irrigation, drinking water, or water conservation.

Some might argue that natural lakes are superior to artificial ones because they are as nature created them. I will not argue that point because there are few things that equal the beauty of a natural lake. However, there are many merits to reservoirs besides the fact that Utah has them in abundance.

First, a reservoir is maintained and accessible. Very often there is a staff employed to ensure the water remains clean and to monitor the dam and water levels. This means that there will be a maintained road for access.

Next, a reservoir is often unique. Natural lakes follow the lines created by nature. The reservoir follows a dictated and engineered design. Thus a reservoir appears in locations where you might not expect to find a lake. Valleys, canyons, and even deserts suddenly become paddle destinations.

Reservoirs often have amenities. As these places are public lands, access for everyone is allowed and even encouraged. To accommodate the visitors, there are campsites, picnic grounds, rest rooms, and boat ramps. In addition, many reservoirs are stocked with fish. Using a reservoir, you can really get the utmost experience from a paddle.

Lake

I have chosen to differentiate a reservoir from a lake in this book. Both are standing bodies of water fed by rivers and have similar features.

However, the key difference is that a lake is a natural formation. Utah has very few natural lakes, and thus, you will not see it mentioned often.

There is not much reason to note the difference because from a paddling perspective, there is little difference. However, I have chosen to point it out more for interest. As the landscape is dotted with both constructed and natural formations, it is nice to know on whose work you are playing.

Keep in mind that while there are many natural lakes in Utah, some have been dammed to increase the size and ensure that water will be held for a longer period of time. I will still identify these as natural lakes, but they have water management involved in their designs.

River

Utah has a few beautiful and majestic rivers, but where do you start and end your guide to a river? Most, if not all, the rivers in the state travel across the borders over hundreds of miles and exist in varying sizes and forms as they undulate across the landscape.

The rivers noted in this book are specific areas that I see as favorable flatwater paddle trips. The distance and specifics about these river excursions are noted. However, there are excellent opportunities to put in and paddle at other locations. These are simply locations that I know work.

DIFFICULTY

Because this book is primarily focused on flatwater paddling, difficulty is sort of relative. Factors like weather, traffic, winds, etc., all contribute to the complexity of a particular body of water. Thus, the difficulty noted here specifically identifies those factors that contribute to the challenge the water might offer an inexperienced paddler.

Consider the symbols on a ski slope or for a film rating. You get a starting baseline and guidance as to what you might encounter when taking on the next level. This idea is implemented here with the same care and consideration. Here are guidelines to consider when reading the difficulty level noted:

Easy
Small- to medium-sized body of water
Sheltered
Low incidence of wake or chop
Little or no powerboat traffic
Limited use
Simple portage
Available shoreline
Limited potential weather issues

Moderate
Medium- to large-sized body of water
Partly sheltered
Some wake or chop at varying times
Limited powerboat traffic
Moderate use
Moderate portage
Limited shoreline
Some potential weather issues

Difficult
Large-sized body of water
No shelter
Frequent wake or chop
Regular powerboat traffic
Heavy use
Difficult portage
No shoreline
Many potential weather issues

Of course, it will be rare for a body of water to exhibit all of the characteristics in one category. However, each paddle was measured based on these criteria. If a body of water has multiple aspects in one category, then that will be the difficulty rating provided. If there are factors that deviate from the criteria, they will be noted.

SEASON

"To every season, turn, turn, turn." Those words, from the biblical book Ecclesiastes and made famous by the Byrds, certainly weren't referencing paddling but are wholly appropriate for this situation. Utah has four beautiful seasons. However, depending on where you are and your altitude, the seasons can turn, turn, turn.

In the north, you can anticipate paddling typically in the spring, summer, and autumn. In some cases, you may even be able to paddle into the winter. Specific issues regarding the season and the body of water will be noted if they impact paddling.

In the south, paddling is available year-round. In fact, I have paddled in late October in southern Utah, and it is beautiful. Yet it is important to consider the kind of gear you'll need and the type of paddling you might be doing in the colder months. The weather can get chilly, especially at night; temperatures in desert regions drop quickly after dark.

Seasons noted are intended as general guidelines, and weather reports should always be consulted before any trip on the water. I have paddled comfortably on the Great Salt Lake in December, and I've been freezing cold on the Colorado in Moab in March. You have to use good judgment.

Above 7,000 feet, all bets are off. The weather is wetter and cooler, with snow possible in the mountains even during the summer. In addition, Utah has a unique, yet common, phenomenon called an inversion. Basically, a weather system gets trapped in the valley and temperatures rise in the mountains, which equals a sunny spring day up high and bitter cold down below.

SIZE

Of all the technical measurements provided in this book, this is one that can really fluctuate from year to year. As noted, many of the destinations in this book are reservoirs and are part of a water system. Thus, depending on the prior year's snowfall and water consumption in the community, the dimension of each location can vary significantly.

In a drought year, some bodies of water become very low and decrease in acreage. In wet years, size can increase, and in the case of rivers, the level of difficulty can change. Sizes are provided in acres for reservoirs and lakes. Rivers are given in miles based upon the trip being described; width and flow are provided in the Paddle Overview.

DIRECTIONS

Where do you start? In a state as large as Utah, it is difficult to establish a particular starting point for directions. I could have arbitrarily selected Salt Lake City, the capital and center of most of the state's population. However, that would mean many of the more remote locations would have pages and pages of directions.

In most situations, I have included directions from the closest city or town. These towns are of relatively notable size. In addition, they are much easier to spot on a map than a road intersection or noted park. Last, providing the city also gives you a point to work from in terms of arranging accommodations and finding services.

It is always best to consult a good map or use your GPS when trying to locate any of the bodies of water noted in this book. I have done my best to ensure the directions are clear and simple. However, using those tools will provide a better perspective and make getting to the locales much simpler.

PUT-IN

I am always concerned about providing a launch site. You see, in some ways, I am very lazy. I would rather not portage, and I simply love a nice shore where I can conveniently prepare for an afternoon float. Thus, my selected put-ins are focused on these qualities.

The problem with most, if not all, of the locations is that they are based upon my travels at the time of writing the book. Because of irrigation use, the water levels change, and what might have been a good put-in now becomes a challenging launch spot.

You may arrive at any of the listed waters and draw a conclusion that I am nuts. The fact is, I could not circumnavigate every body of water looking for a put-in. I picked what seemed obvious and easy. However, you know your boat, your strength, and what you are willing to do to get into the water.

When possible, I have noted boat ramps or shore locations that seem ideal. I have also identified any permanent landmarks.

OTHER SPORTS

This book is focused on paddling. Yet it is a sport that goes well with many others activities. While on your paddling trip, you might want to take an opportunity to hike, observe wildlife, or drop a line in the water. Some of the other sports I will note include fishing, camping, swimming, bird-watching, and hiking.

Of course, there might be other sporting opportunities available in an area. Skiing or biking comes to mind. However, the sports noted here coincide with paddling. I doubt too many people will pack a pair of skis in their kayak, but a few will certainly bring along a fishing pole or a pair of binoculars.

INFORMATION

Whenever possible, I have tried to provide an additional resource beyond the book so you can get current information. Print is static, but Mother Nature is not. It is advisable that you check out the locations before your visit.

For example, while visiting Big Sand Wash, I discovered that they had drained the reservoir and were rebuilding the dam. When I made my stop, there was no information on the construction, and I had not bothered to call before I arrived.

For each location I have tried to provide either a good Web site or telephone number. I have tested and verified this data. My hope and expectation is that much of this book will not change over time and that it will be useful for years to come.

While on a paddling trip, you might want to drop a line in the water.

PADDLE OVERVIEW

Providing a detailed description of the water and surrounding landscape, the Paddle Overview attempts to paint a picture of the paddle experience. My emphasis is on what makes the paddle special. As I visited each of these destinations, I tried to capture the exciting, interesting, and emotional elements.

Whenever possible, I note features to explore by boat and the potential water conditions. Naturally, the weather dictates a lot of what the experience will bring. However, I comment on the likelihood of wind and the impact of extraneous factors such as other users.

Because this book is for us outdoorsy types who want to spend time communing with nature, campsites are noted. However, I also believe that a nice hotel is a simpler form of camping, and I recognize that some people prefer a nice restaurant to eating s'mores by a fire at night.

When listing accommodations, I provide those closest to the destination and then make note of any towns or locations that might provide comfortable and clean motels or hotels. If I know of specific locations to stay near or at the destination, they will also be mentioned.

It is important to remember that many of the places covered in the book are popular and will require reservations or early arrival. On holiday weekends, you may need to turn up on a Thursday to get that campsite you want or pay for a day or two that you are not there in order to save your spot.

If your plans include a stay in a hotel, you may also want to consider making a reservation. A number of the locations are near small rural towns. These places may have only one or two hotels and those can become promptly booked with a rush of tourists.

OTHER DESTINATIONS

At the end of every region, I have noted "Other Destinations" and made some brief comments about each. These locations did not make the cut when considering what was a "Best Bet" for the region. While some are excellent sites, they may be missing a few, or many, of the best qualities that the featured destinations have.

For example, a reservoir may have stunning scenery and marvelous conditions, but the access road requires a four-wheel-drive vehicle. Or perhaps the place is loaded with powerboats and personal watercraft.

Paddling against the current on the Bear River.

This scenario was a typical reason for excluding them from the top of my list.

Of course, these are my opinions. One of your personal favorites may be listed under "Other Destinations." Please do not take it personally as many of these places were close runners up to the top spots. In all, these destinations may be worth your time, but you might have to weigh other factors if you choose to visit. The elements listed with each of the other destinations include name, county, longitude/latitude, size, directions, and comment.

The Regions

PART II

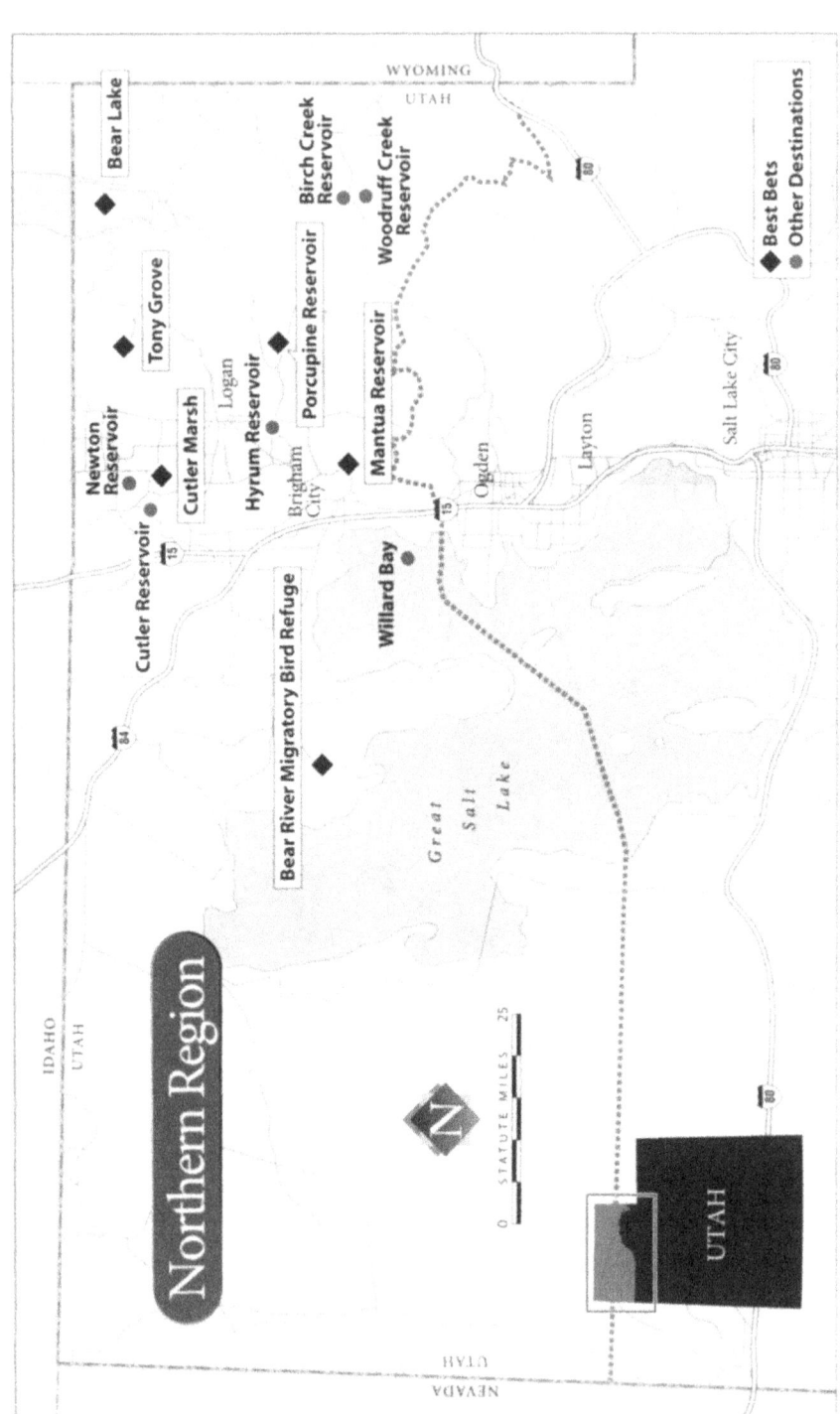

CHAPTER 3

Summer vacationers are drawn to Bear Lake, a popular destination in the Northern Region.

Northern Region

Distinguished by abundant national forest and green mountains, the Northern Region of Utah is a pastoral setting complete with grazing cows, snow-capped peaks, and lush valleys. This fertile farmland pairs with the lakes and rivers of this region to make a great destination for paddlers.

The two largest cities in the region are Logan and Brigham City. Logan is the larger of the two. Home to Utah State University, it has all the trappings of a college town. During the summer months, Logan hosts a thriving art community with the local opera company and a festival celebrating the American West.

Logan and the surrounding communities are called Cache Valley, which has a history based in trapping. Early explorers found abundant furred animals in the region and made it central to their hunting. In fact, the name Cache was coined by the trappers as they hunted and stored the pelts gathered during the winter months. While paddling the region, it is not uncommon to see beaver, fox, and rabbit.

Two canyon drives are featured in the region. A drive up Logan Canyon is often breathtaking. Massive gray cliffs, stone monoliths, and groves of quaking aspens await you. Logan Canyon, a national scenic byway, offers winding curves and a stunning drive any time of the year.

Bear Lake, located at the north end of the canyon, is a popular destination for summer vacationers. Its long sandy beaches, large size, and various resorts draw people from all over the region. The lake is a cool reprieve from the summer heat, and the place buzzes with activity. You can find dinner theater, outdoor movies, and a lot of other fun activities.

Summers at Bear Lake are also noted for their raspberries. These deeply colored berries grow large and in abundance around the lake and are harvested to make a variety of concoctions. Jams, jellies, and muffins are very popular. Yet of all the forms that this fruit can take, the raspberry shake is the most celebrated.

Both Garden City and Laketown are noted for their drive-in restaurants, where you can get a delicious raspberry shake fresh and made to order. A throwback to the restaurants of the 1950s, most dining is outside, and you walk up to the window to order. The prices are relatively cheap, and the food is a bit on the greasy side, but very tasty.

Now, many define a shake as a drinkable form of ice cream. However, these raspberry shakes will cause a lung to collapse if you attempt to slurp it through a straw. Made with soft-serve ice cream, the shakes are blended with the ingredients you select, and you are provided a lengthy spoon to consume it.

On the south end of Logan is Sardine Canyon. This is another beautiful drive. Connecting Brigham City and Logan, it is noted for its narrow spots and harsh winter conditions. However, it also an incredible spot to view the autumn colors. The canyon is named Sardine not because it is narrow, but because of the small, sardine-like fish caught there by early settlers.

Brigham City is the smaller of the two cities in the region. Famous for its peaches and small-town charm, Brigham is a page right out of old-town America. The city's main street and historic structures are worthy of a diversion from the interstate. If you visit just after Labor Day, it has a huge Peach Days celebration.

Just south of Brigham City on US 89 is evidence of the rural heritage of the Northern Region. Along this passage resides a variety of fruit farms and stands. These places provide fresh, locally grown produce from spring through autumn. Few things are better than a fresh apple on a crisp autumn day.

The Northern Region has built its heritage on agriculture and industry. Even today, that culture exists and is practiced. As you drive this area, note the 4H clubs, farmland, horses, cattle, and countryside. It is a delightful spot for a day in your canoe or kayak.

BEST BETS

BEAR LAKE
County: Rich
LONG/LAT: N41 53.090 W111 21.806
Elevation: 5,901 feet/1,799 meters
Body Type: Lake
Difficulty: Difficult. Large lake with heavy chop, constant winds, and shifting weather.
Season: Late spring, summer, early autumn
Size: 69,760 acres
Directions: Follow US 89 in Logan by turning right on 400 North Street. Take the road up Logan Canyon about 40 miles. The signs for Logan Canyon and Bear Lake are well marked.

Bear Lake is a challenging paddle.

Put-in: There is abundant shoreline for launching from a beach. However, the lake also hosts three different state parks with complete marinas and boat launches.
Other Sports: Fishing, camping, swimming
Information: www.bearlake.org

Paddle Overview
Your first view of Bear Lake as you come over the mountains shines of azure. The captivating blue lures you down to its shores like a siren and beckons to be paddled. However, as with a siren, there is potential risk. From the abundant boaters to the unpredictable weather, this lake can be full of hazards (even supernatural ones).

Let me begin by stating that Bear Lake is an excellent place to paddle. It is large, open, and full of opportunities to really give those arms a workout. It has great beaches and an abundant shoreline. In addition, there are ample facilities to accommodate short or lengthy visits. Yet it remains a challenging spot.

Bear Lake is usually choppy. The wind seems to always blow, which makes it a popular destination for sailboats. In addition, there are abundant powerboaters and watercraft riders. Because of this activity, the water can churn with whitecaps even on calm weather days.

Bear Lake is also very cold. In the shallows during the summer, the water is pleasant, but out in the middle, it is deep, dark, and frigid. If you were to capsize, you will definitely get a chill. During the late summer or early spring, you might even be at risk for hypothermia.

Last, Bear Lake's weather can be unpredictable. I have spent a lot of time on this lake over the years, and I have seen it turn ugly in a short period of time. The surrounding mountains hide impending weather patterns, and before you know it, the swells start to rise.

If these concerns do not sway you, you may want to consider that the lake is home to a monster. Yes, for more than 160 years, rumors have spread that the lake is inhabited by its own version of Nessie. I am going to assume that it lives on the Idaho side because I have not seen it on my paddles.

With all these challenges, Bear Lake is still a wonderful lake to paddle. It is vast and provides a fantastic test for the experienced or novice paddler alike. Strength and endurance are required to cover its length. Few other lakes in Utah can match its size and beauty.

TONY GROVE

County: Cache
LONG/LAT: N40 .183117 W111 .027550
Elevation: 8,043 feet/2,452 meters
Body Type: Lake
Difficulty: Easy. This is a very small natural lake in a protected area.

Tony Grove, a paddle at 8,000 feet, has glacial formations and snow-capped peaks.

Season: Summer only

Size: 25 acres

Directions: From Logan, follow US 89 up Logan Canyon approximately 20 miles to the Tony Grove Lake turnoff on the left. Continue 7 miles up this canyon to the Tony Grove parking lot. The lake is about 100 feet from the lot when the water is high.

Put-in: Depending on the water level, much of the shore is available. There is a short portage from the parking lot to the water but nothing too difficult.

Other Sports: Fishing, camping, bird-watching, hiking

Information: 435-755-3620

Paddle Overview

Tony Grove is far more about the journey than the actual destination. This small natural lake, located at the top of the Bear River Range, has a pristine and perfect natural setting. However, it is not very large and certainly not challenging in any fashion. This begs the question as to why would someone go to the trouble to haul a boat up a mountain for this relatively small body of water.

What pushes someone to paddle this place is the setting. It is not often that you can paddle at 8,000 feet. The epic glacial formations, snow-capped peaks, and majestic pines are intoxicating. Massive cliffs and boulders decorate the lake's edge, and you will find few settings that equal this beauty.

Tony Grove is a simple paddle with simple pleasures. The icy cool water is a wonderful reprieve from a hot summer day. It is a quiet location surrounded by wildlife and breathtaking scenery. While there may not be much challenge in its waters, there is something to enjoy.

Because the mountains shelter the lake, its surface is smooth and reflective. Any boat will work here, but you may find it more convenient to take a lightweight recreational boat or a ducky. You will probably want to dress warmly as temperatures are significantly cooler at that elevation.

In all, make Tony Grove a short trip with a small boat when you are more focused on being in the mountains than on the water. It will be an excellent day.

PORCUPINE RESERVOIR

County: Cache
LONG/LAT: N41 31.010 W111 44.080
Elevation: 5,381 feet/1,640 meters
Body Type: Reservoir
Difficulty: Easy. Light winds could provide a challenge.
Season: Spring, summer, autumn
Size: 77 acres
Directions: From Logan, head south on US 89. Take a left onto UT 165. Follow it south until you get into Paradise. In Paradise, take a left (east) onto 9100 South. Go four blocks, then turn right on UT 162 and follow it into the town of Avon. The road takes a turn to the west. Follow it until 800 East. Take a right onto 800 East, travel about 200 yards, and take a left on La Plata (Canyon Road). Follow that up to the reservoir. There are signs along the way.
Put-in: The north side of the reservoir has camping spots with varying shoreline depending on the water level. More industrious drivers may want to continue to the east end where the shore is not as steep.
Other Sports: Fishing, camping, bird-watching, swimming
Information: Porcupine is excluded from some maps.

Paddle Overview

You have to go through Paradise to get to a kind of paradise. Porcupine Reservoir, near the city of Paradise, sits at the top of a winding road in what seems like a hidden canyon. As you ascend, a tree-lined road provides shade and envelops you in mystery. Until you crest, you can't see the grandeur of this location.

Little Bear River cascades into Porcupine Reservoir.

Porcupine is a tremendous site filled with many interesting features for a day out on the water. For starters, the surrounding mountains are abrupt and provide limited shoreline. However, this provides excellent spots of protected water, which allows you to paddle with ease.

Along the western shore, the Little Bear River empties into the reservoir like a cascading waterfall or fountain. The rush of water from this mountain stream creates a restful sound and an interesting feature to explore. In addition, few of the limited beaches are not far and make nice breaks from paddling.

There are two dominant forks to the canyon. The main exists down the middle with some nice curving shoreline to paddle in and out of. On our visit, we found a fine little inlet on the north shore where the water was suitable for put-ins and swimming. It was a great launch spot.

The wind gets going a bit close to the dam, but I did not find it sufficiently troublesome to consider it a big problem. There are areas with small tree coverage, which lure birds to fish and nest. On the south side, the area is less accessible to people; while the shore is steep, I am certain you might catch some moose or elk coming for a drink.

Porcupine is not as easy to access as nearby Hyrum State Park. This means you will have the benefits of few people, no wake, and lovely scenery. What more could you want from a paddle?

MANTUA RESERVOIR

County: Cache
LONG/LAT: N41 30.177 W111 56.548
Elevation: 5,159 feet/1,572 meters
Body Type: Reservoir
Difficulty: Very easy
Season: Spring, summer, autumn
Size: 225 acres
Directions: From Brigham City, follow 1100 South heading east until you start up the canyon. At the top of the canyon, you will see signs. Take a right onto West 100 South into town. Take a left onto

The open water of Mantua is typically smooth and calm.

Main Street and head north a few blocks. The reservoir is on the right.

Put-in: On the west side of the reservoir, there is a boat launch and pier. It doesn't get any easier than this.

Other Sports: Fishing, bird-watching, swimming

Information: None

Paddle Overview

Mantua is a very sensible place. From its kidney shape to the small town nestled on its shores, the place evokes practicality. Smooth surfaced and scenic, Mantua is a pleasure in every respect. In fact, there is not a thing difficult about it except the pronunciation of its name.

Mantua (pronounced *man-away*) is a small- to medium-sized reservoir located in between Brigham City and Logan. In a pristine valley surrounded by mountains, the whole place reeks of perfection. Whether you are picnicking in the clean little park or fishing from the shore, Mantua is an idyllic spot for a paddle.

In many ways it achieves perfection. The place is very accessible. It has a great boat dock with an excellent pier. There is a nice-sized surface area that can be a quick paddle before going into work or an entire day excursion on the water. It has a charming little general store in town for supplies and snacks.

On the south side, you will find a marshy area that you can explore. Trees and marsh combine to make a perfect nesting spot for a variety of migratory birds. Also, depending on the water level, you will find a lot of little twists and turns to explore in your boat.

On the open water, conditions at Mantua are typically smooth and calm. However, powerboats are allowed, and on weekends, you might find some traffic and the chop left in their wake. I prefer to sneak away for a midweek paddle. On most occasions, you will find few other paddlers or be entirely alone.

On the eastern shore, you will discover a large grassy knoll that is very enticing to climb. In fact, it is so enticing that I have done it myself. However, I later learned that this is a popular nesting spots for rattlesnakes. In addition, it is not public property, though the local farmers do not enforce the boundaries.

Mantua is not the most challenging spot nor is it riddled with nooks to explore. There is nothing distinguishable about it, yet it is an enticing place to visit and lures you to paddle it when you trek through the canyon. Be sensible and make it a stop on your journeys through this region.

BEAR RIVER MIGRATORY BIRD REFUGE

County: Box Elder
LONG/LAT: N41 28.452 W112 10.629
Elevation: 4,205 feet/1,282 meters
Body Type: River
Difficulty: Easy to moderate. Paddling upstream is a challenge in the spring.
Season: Spring, summer, autumn
Size: 3–5 miles
Directions: The Bear River Migratory Bird Refuge is located 50 miles north of Salt Lake City via I-15. Take exit 366 (Forest Street) in Brigham City. Follow Forest Street west for 14 miles to the refuge entrance.
Put-in: The best put-in is just inside the entrance of the bird refuge. Parking and a small visitors center are available. You can paddle upstream for a while and turn around when you have completed your exploration. An alternate put-in is in the city of Corrine. However, this is a lengthy six-hour paddle to the refuge.
Other Sports: Bird-watching, hiking
Information: www.bearriver.fws.gov

Paddle Overview

The expression "one for the birds" has an interesting meaning when discussing this location. A single day on the river can yield hundreds of bird sightings. As the name suggests, the Bear River Migratory Bird Refuge is a stop for birds migrating throughout the year. Literally thousands flock here annually while they make their treks north and south.

For the paddler who is fond of birds, there is not a better place to find them, watch them, and experience such remarkable varieties. As you paddle along, you will encounter pelicans, ibises, herons, and 50 other species. Be certain to bring a good pair of binoculars and your camera.

The refuge is fed by the Bear River. This strange square-shaped river touches both the mountain slopes and the western plains of Utah. Over 300 miles long, the river originates in the High Uintas, treks north into

Ibis, one of the many bird species you'll see at Bear River's refuge

Wyoming and Idaho, and finally takes a sharp bend south into Cache and Box Elder counties. At the south end of the river's journey, a massive wetland oasis is created as it flows into the Great Salt Lake.

The Bear River Migratory Bird Refuge is a 74,000-acre national wildlife refuge. Made up of marshlands, rivers, ponds, open water, and mudflats, it is an important spot for waterfowl through the entire year. In addition, the whole area is an important ecosystem that is a critical for wildlife in Utah.

Before you take your boat out to the refuge, it is important to note that *you can't actually paddle within its boundaries*. The wetlands are protected for the birds. However, you can still enjoy it if you plan your trip properly.

I enjoy bringing my boat just inside the entrance of the refuge and parking my car. There is an easy put-in, and I then paddle upstream. The flow of the Bear River is hardly noticeable at this point. The current in the spring can offer a challenge, but by the end of summer, you can make it with little difficulty.

Taking your boat 2 to 3 miles upstream will give you the experience of the refuge without violating its rules. In addition, the meandering nature of the river will take you in and out of rookeries, nesting areas, and other rich birding locations. The grassy shoreline provides excellent cover so the birds might not immediately notice you.

Be forewarned, slow-moving rivers and marshlands are not just great homes for nesting birds. Smaller flying creatures such as gnats and mosquitoes are plentiful, and you will want to have doused yourself in your favorite bug spray before setting foot in your boat.

As you paddle upstream, you will note a lot of the farming heritage that has existed in these wetlands for generations. Old tractors and implements decorate the landscape. Barns and livestock are interspersed in the massive fields of marsh. You can also observe the water management canals and irrigation channels that have existed for more than a century.

In addition, hunting is a very popular sport here. In fact, the refuge, through the state, issues permits to duck hunters every autumn to help manage the population of waterfowl. You will see many aspects of the hunting community including lodges, duck blinds, and even the occasional hunter scouting out his seasonal plans.

You will also want to note that the area is sensitive to water levels. In the spring, it is not uncommon for the paddling to take on a whole new dimension. You will want to be careful because what may seem like a viable route could actually be floodwaters that have created a new and unexpected branch with a dead end.

The Bear is a river that twists and turns for miles through this area, and in the end you may paddle long but not travel far. On one occasion, I spent three hours in my canoe only to have paddled about 4 miles as the crow flies. Oh, did I mention the refuge is home to crows as well?

CUTLER MARSH

County: Cache
LONG/LAT: N41 44.793 W111 57.164
Elevation: 4,402 feet/1,342 meters
Body Type: Lake
Difficulty: Moderate. Acres and acres of marshy maze.
Season: Spring, summer, autumn
Size: 10,000 acres
Directions: From Logan, follow US 89 to East 200 North (UT 30). Follow East 200 North west for approximate 6 miles. The launch is on your left.
Put-in: There are actually five different designated launches that can be used as a put-in. The most convenient is at the small marina.
Other Sports: Fishing, bird-watching, hiking
Information: www.bridgerlandaudubon.org/wetlandsmaze

Paddle Overview
Wetlands are fairly uncommon in Utah. The arid landscape and small number of rivers means that those places are distinctive and important to the survival of the migratory bird species that stop as they travel north and south annually. Thus, Cutler Marsh is an exceptional place that every paddler should experience and enjoy.

Perhaps one of the most interesting spots in the Northern Region, Cutler Marsh is a must-visit. A paddler can spend hours exploring and experiencing the maze of narrow glens, hidden channels, open water, and of course, marshland. This place is a paddler's dream.

This 10,000-acre wetland was created and is managed by Utah Power, which protects and preserves it. Tall grass, muddy water, and cat-

Relaxing in a spectacular place—the wetlands of Cutler Marsh

tails sway in the breeze; this place induces peace. This serene setting has been created by those who understand the importance of the local ecosystem and environment.

Multiple rookeries are maintained for a variety of species inside the marsh. Ibises, herons, egrets, and pelicans are among the many birds that make their home here. On a good day, you will see all of these birds and more traversing these vast waters.

Cutler is a completely unique location because the management of the marsh includes specific designs for the purpose of paddling. There are canoe trails that permit paddlers to explore the marsh and its inhabitants while testing navigation skills. Strict regulations prevent the use of powerboats, and wakeless speeds are enforced.

There are immeasurable paddle routes you can navigate, which is why the marsh is a labyrinth in every sense of the word. Paddling in Cutler encourages and invites discovery. Every turn reveals a new and wondrous surprise. Experienced paddlers and novices alike will find a feeling of joy at every bend.

On calm days, the surface of the water reflects the surrounding mountains. On a windy day, the open areas can develop mild chop, but nothing too powerful. The water is relatively shallow in most areas, and if you are swamped, you can simply stand up and get back in your boat.

I suggest using a GPS unless you have an excellent sense of direction. The scale of Cutler, combined with limited visibility and few distinguishing landmarks, challenges even the best navigators. While you might see an occasional dead tree or interesting looking bush, one area of tall grass begins to resemble another and soon you have lost your way.

If you do not own a GPS, do not be discouraged. Proper precautions can mitigate the risk of going astray. Be certain to note any features as you paddle and then recall them later to retrace your route back to your put-in. The canoe trails have some markers, but these have weathered over time; I have had a difficult time locating them since my last visit.

You will be presently surprised how easy Cutler Marsh is to access. There are multiple locations to put in and explore. One ideal location is just a short drive from downtown Logan, just off UT 30. A small marina and pier specifically designed for canoes and kayaks await you. In addition, there is a picnic area with rest rooms.

Access is also available to the north and to the east from the Logan River. Each of these provides equal ease of entry. Wherever you choose to paddle, it really doesn't matter. With its beautiful scenery and endless paddle options, any spot on Cutler Marsh is a special place that should not be missed.

OTHER DESTINATIONS

BIRCH CREEK RESERVOIR
County: Rich
LONG/LAT: N41 30.461 W111 18.702
Size: 63 acres
Directions: Take UT 39 from Woodruff for about 6 miles. Just past the cattle guard, you will see a sign on the right. Follow the dirt road about 1 mile.
Comment: Birch Creek is actually two paddle spots. One small location exists below the dam and is not too impressive. The paddling upstream of the dam is nice, but you have to be willing to climb and slide for a put-in. I call it a motivational paddle.

CUTLER RESERVOIR
County: Cache
LONG/LAT: N41 47.216 W111 57.238
Size: 350 acres
Directions: Take UT 30 west and turn north on UT 23. Turn east at the south end of the lake for Benson Marina. This is north of the marsh and south of the actual reservoir.
Comment: Big brother to Cutler Marsh, this reservoir is mostly frequented by anglers and powerboaters. Keep your canoe or kayak in wetland areas if you want to avoid the traffic.

HYRUM RESERVOIR
County: Cache
LONG/LAT: N41 37.688 W111 52.010
Size: 264 acres

Directions: From Logan, follow US 89 south to UT 101. Make a left on UT 101 heading east into Hyrum. The road takes a sharp turn to the right. Follow the signs straight into the park.

Comment: This well-accommodated state park is mostly focused on people with watercraft and powerboats. However, there are suitable paddle spots on the east end of the reservoir. In all, this is a nice clean spot that is convenient and paddle worthy.

NEWTON RESERVOIR

County: Cache
LONG/LAT: N41 27.928 W111 19.175
Size: 350 acres

Directions: From Logan, go north on US 91. Make a left onto UT 218 and follow it into town. Take a right onto North 100 West. Follow that north to 9000 North and take a right. The road makes a bend to the right, and there are signs. Follow the road to the reservoir.

Comment: The first reservoir created by Mormon settlers, Newton is a quiet, out-of-the-way spot. It has a large surface area, and while the scenery is sparse, it is a decent spot to paddle.

WILLARD BAY

County: Box Elder
LONG/LAT: N41 25.302 W112 03.206
Size: 9,900 acres

Directions: Take I-15 to Willard Bay (exit 360).

Comment: Willard is big—very big. It has very nice facilities and clean beaches. However, it is not a particular favorite of mine for paddling. Because of its large powerboat use and the prevailing winds, the place is very choppy. The fact that it is exceptionally close to the interstate and has a complete lack of scenery makes it one I pass often and never paddle.

WOODRUFF CREEK RESERVOIR

County: Rich

LONG/LAT: N41 27.928 W111 19.175

Size: 90 acres

Directions: Take UT 39 from Woodruff for about 5 miles. The dirt road is on the left. The 7-mile journey is rough, and the road climbs up some narrow sections to the dam. There is easy access to the reservoir once you are over the dam.

Comment: While Woodruff is not impressive, it has a nice, subtle shoreline and a decent surface area. But the rough road makes it a destination for only the really motivated paddler. If you have a decent four-wheel-drive vehicle, you may want to try it for its relative isolation.

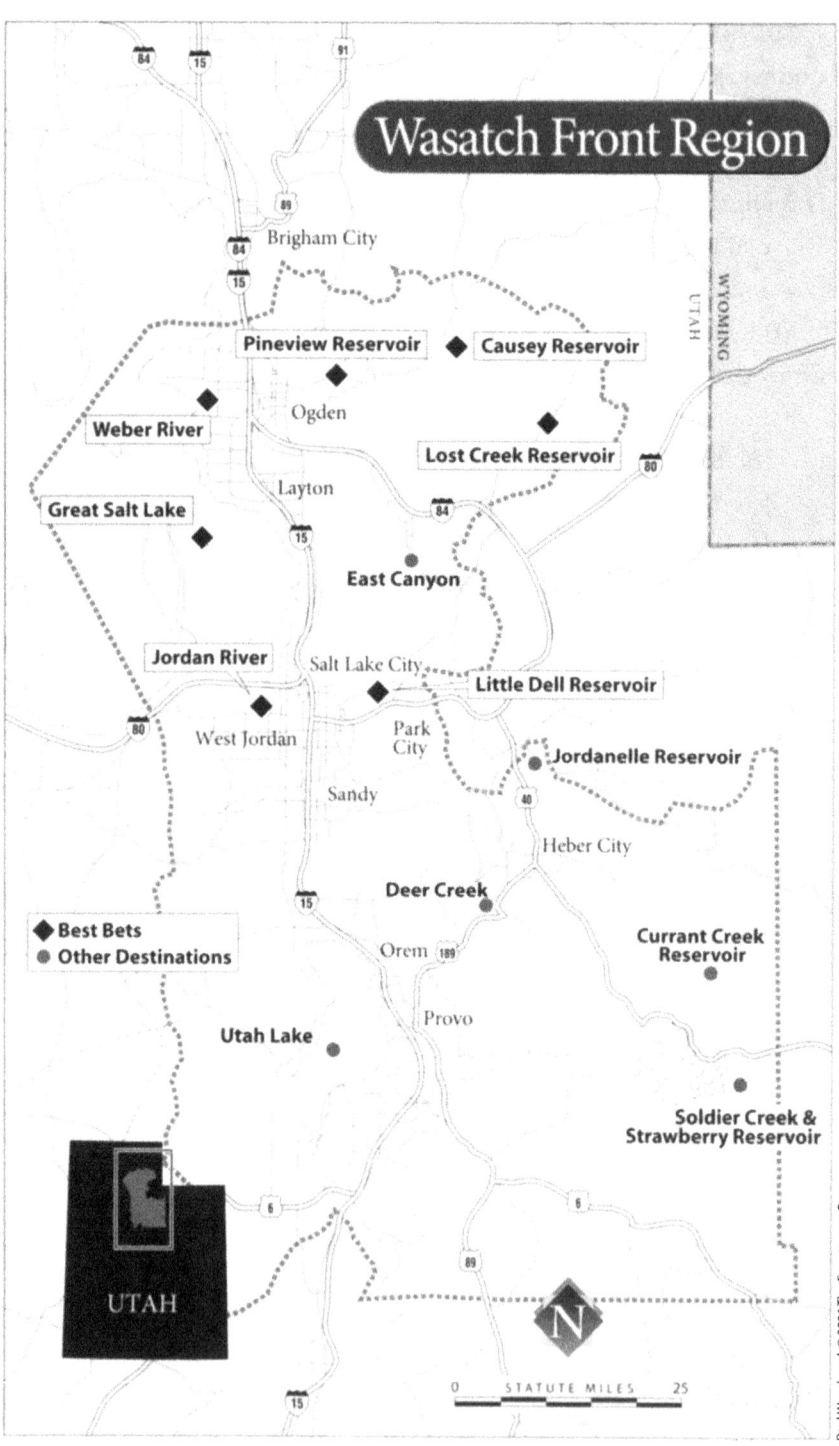

CHAPTER 4

Downtown Salt Lake City is a hub of activity and home to the Mormon Church.

Wasatch Front Region

Stretching nearly 150 miles, the Wasatch Front is the activity hub of the state. This region accounts for 75 percent of Utah's population, but represents only 7 percent of the land mass. It has been the central urban region of the state for more than 150 years. Yet even with all this population and activity, it still holds many paddling treasures.

The best attribute of this region is that in a relatively short time, you can escape the urban landscape for a mountain lake or river trip. There are many excellent paddles located very close, and some are arguably as good as the more rural locales. Just like the skiing, paddling is just a short jaunt over a mountain pass or up a canyon.

Of course, the most notable municipality in this region is Salt Lake City. In the state's capital and cultural center, you can find all the amenities of any large city. The city offers the best in restaurants, music, theater, and the arts. Throughout the year, the place is buzzing with activity and opportunities.

Salt Lake has a strong sports culture. It is home to several professional sports teams, world-class skiing, extraordinary mountain hikes, and renowned rock climbing. In addition, it played host to the 2002 Olympic Winter Games. Of course, paddling is no exception, and you will find some terrific settings close by.

Salt Lake has been working diligently to breathe life into its downtown. Many of the city activities are centered in this area. Its history is closely tied to the Mormons, and the church has its headquarters and center downtown. No matter where you are staying in the city, you can easily access all the fun activities in the city center with a ride on the light-rail public transit.

Directly north of Salt Lake is Davis County. It is strange that Salt Lake City has earned its name considering very little of the city or county borders the lake. The people of Davis can view the lake from many locations in the county, and they have most of the best lake access as well.

Davis County is one of the fastest growing spots in the state. A large air-force base and the county's proximity to Salt Lake and Ogden have helped growth in the once rural communities. Davis County thrives with business and is home to the state's only amusement park.

If you hear people speaking about lagoon, know that it is not a place to paddle, but rather a century-old location for people of all ages to enjoy. From spring through autumn, this park entertains with thrill rides and stage shows. It is a popular spot for locals and a great place for the kids.

North of Davis is Ogden. This smaller city has a long tradition of social and community diversity. It could be considered the black sheep of Utah. Unlike the rest of the state, Ogden's history is not tied to the original Mormon pioneers. It has been a hub of activity since its early days.

Explorers settled the first territorial outpost in the state at the confluence of the Ogden and Weber rivers. Later, the outpost became a central switching location for trains connecting to the west. In fact, the gold spike driven into the earth at the connection of the transcontinental railroad in 1869 is only an hour north. Last, Ogden is a taste of the Old West and maintains this heritage through activities and architecture.

Downtown you will find historic 25th Street and buildings that date back to the late nineteenth century. The street has a nice collection of restaurants and bars, along with a lot of charm. At the end of the block, the Union Station has several fascinating museums, including a Browning gun museum. Browning was founded in the area and is still operated nearby. During the summer, Ogden maintains old-fashioned outdoor rodeos, and police officers patrol on horseback.

To the south of Salt Lake, you have Utah County. This is the second most populous region of the state, and it continues to grow. In recent years, the Provo and Orem areas have developed to be almost a single metropolis. While they are two distinct cities, the boundaries are indiscernible.

Provo is most notably home to Brigham Young University. However, it also has a lot to offer those recreating in the area. Timpanogos Cave National Monument, only a short trip north, is a fascinating place to visit. Located high on the side of a mountain and accessed by a long hike, the cave has been explored for more than one hundred years.

Also north of Provo you can find Thanksgiving Point. These notable grounds were created in 2000 and combine 50 acres of beautiful themed gardens. In addition, the area hosts a golf course and a massive dinosaur museum.

The soaring mountains of Utah County hold a number of great surprises. A short drive east from Provo is a beautiful canyon and the Sundance Resort. Actor Robert Redford, who created the renowned Sundance Film Festival, owns this trendy rustic resort. He has used the resort as a destination that celebrates the arts, hosts cultural events, and maintains a social conscience.

At the end of the canyon, you will find the hamlet of Heber City. This quaint city is a popular stop for paddlers on their way to one of the three nearby reservoirs. One of its tourist draws is the Heber Creeper, an old steam engine that pumps smoke from its stack and blows its whistle as it makes its way down Provo Canyon. Rides are a romantic throwback to times past.

Nearby Midway was settled by the Swiss and has maintained the charm of its heritage in both its architecture and events. Every summer it hosts Swiss Days, a celebration that draws crowds from around the state. This small community has grown to become a popular resort area.

The Wasatch Front is the hub of activity for the state of Utah. It is the central gathering spot for culture, art, music, and sports. Virtually everything is right at your fingertips, including some terrific paddling.

BEST BETS

GREAT SALT LAKE
County: Davis
LONG/LAT: N41 03.593 W112 14.321
Elevation: 4,500 feet/1,372 meters
Body Type: Lake
Difficulty: Easy to moderate. Very large paddle area with shifting water conditions.
Season: Spring, summer, autumn, winter
Size: 1,088,000 acres
Directions: From Salt Lake, take I-15 north to the Syracuse exit (#335). Go west 7 miles on UT 108 to the Antelope Island State Park fee booth. The 6-mile-long causeway leads to the island. On the island take your first right, and the marina is on the right.
Put-in: The marina on Antelope Island is an ideal spot. There is parking, a large boat ramp, and full facilities.

Other Sports: Camping, bird-watching, hiking, climbing, swimming
Information: www.utah.com/stateparks/antelope_island; www.great saltlakekayak.com

Paddle Overview

Probably the most recognized body of water in Utah, the Great Salt Lake is a massive remnant of ancient sea. The largest U.S. lake west of the Mississippi River, it is the fourth largest inland terminal in the world and the largest migratory bird stop in the West. It is a natural wonderland that is best explored by paddling.

The Great Salt Lake is distinctive in many ways. It has one of the highest salt contents of any body of water on the earth. Also, the lake is a constantly changing entity. Its size shifts significantly throughout the year. This makes finding a consistent put-in difficult.

There are an assortment of marinas, bays, and beaches that are suitable to put in. However, what appears to have water may be dried up farther out. Of all the places I have tried, one that remains steadfast with the changing water levels is the marina on Antelope Island.

Antelope Island, the largest land mass within the lake, is a state park. It is the home of wild bison herds, deer, and of course, antelope. The fascinating landscape, decorated with barren slopes and rocky cliffs, makes the trip out to the island worthwhile in itself.

Paddling is well suited to Antelope. It has a large marina with a nice boat dock, plentiful parking, and other services. In fact, there is a kayak rental shop that provides boats, paddles, and tours of the area directly around the island. From the marina, the paddle conditions are ideal. Because of the brine shrimp industry, water and access to paddling are usually available.

In the late 1980s, the lake grew to record height and actually exceeded its perceived natural boundaries. In recent times, it has dropped to record lows, exposing huge areas of dry land. Because the level of the lake shifts from year to year, a canoe or kayak is one of the few boats able to consistently explore its wonders.

The Great Salt Lake, probably the most recognized body of water in Utah

Exploration is one of the key attractions. From the marina, there are many places to investigate around Antelope Island. Egg Island, the beaches and rocky shores of Antelope, and the open water of the lake are relatively easy and fascinating paddles.

On a calm day, the lake's surface resembles glass, and you can see the Wasatch Range in its reflection. However, the Great Salt Lake can be a deceptive place, and the weather can turn ugly very quickly. Many people have been lost over the years because of storms that churn up the normally placid lake. It is important to bring your safety gear, check the weather, and paddle with a partner.

Ideal paddle conditions exist in the spring and autumn. The summer is the worst time to visit because both the biting brine flies and the stink of the lake are unforgiving. The winter can be a good time to paddle if temperatures outside are comfortable. I have actually made trips in December and really enjoyed myself.

The Great Salt Lake is an excellent study in ancient history, zoology, and chemistry. The Great Salt Lake is a remnant of Lake Bonneville, a body of water that covered much of what you can see from the lake. The effects of Lake Bonneville's existence are visible on the landscape and surrounding mountains. Water lines, rock formations, and other features take on a new perspective from the Great Salt Lake.

The lake is too saline to support any kind fish or other creatures. However, brine shrimp exist in abundance. These tiny creatures are used for a variety of purposes, and harvesting them is one of the key industries the lake provides. The lake is also home to thousands of migratory birds. Although the lake is considered dead, animal life thrives around it.

The chemistry of the lake is another interesting aspect to explore. To the north and south, companies harvest the plentiful salt that exists within the waters. The constantly shifting chemical balance of the lake causes its waters to change colors. Close observers will note a range of colors, including red, green, blue, and yellow.

The west side of the lake is the home of the Bonneville Salt Flats. The location of famous speed trials, it is one of the smoothest surfaces on the planet. The receding waters of Lake Bonneville created these immense acres of white terrain, which have become a popular destination for filmmakers looking for a surreal spot for car commercials.

In fact, the whole Great Salt Lake experience is surreal. The paddling here has a different dimension than it has at any other place you might visit in the state. Floating on a body of water larger than the state of Rhode Island and practically absent of life brings a strange feeling. It is truly a unique experience.

PINEVIEW RESERVOIR

County: Weber
LONG/LAT: N41 15.848 W111 49.522
Elevation: 4,900 feet/1,494 meters
Body Type: Reservoir
Difficulty: Easy
Season: Spring, summer, autumn, winter
Size: 2,874 acres
Directions: From Salt Lake, take I-15 north to the 12th Street exit in Ogden. Head east on 12th Street (UT 39) up Ogden Canyon for 6 miles. At the top of the dam, make a left. Approximately 0.5 mile on the right is a forest service parking lot with easy access to the reservoir.
Put-in: There is an ideal beach location on the northwest side of the reservoir. This area is in a no-wake zone and allows paddling into the mouth of the canyon.
Other Sports: Fishing, camping, bird-watching, hiking, swimming
Information: www.ogdencvb.org/pineview.html

Paddle Overview

Among the region's more popular bodies of water, Pineview is a destination for boaters of all sorts. Its convenient location and decent size make it well suited for powerboating, personal watercraft, and other motorized sports. However, Pineview has a lot to offer the paddler as well.

Heading out on Pineview Reservoir, one of the region's most popular bodies of water

Located in Ogden Canyon, Pineview spreads across nearly 3,000 acres of pastoral landscape. Surrounded by mountains and the towns of Huntsville and Eden, the reservoir is a summer destination for a variety of sports, including swimming, camping, waterskiing, and of course, paddling.

During the height of the season, you can find yourself paddling among anchored powerboats, sailboats, fishing boats, wind surfers, and many other kayakers and canoeists. The whole scene is very friendly; you will find that most people are respectful to the rules and treat paddlers like pedestrians of the water. This is especially true in the no-wake zones.

A terrific benefit of Pineview is its layout. The reservoir provides many fingers that are excellent for kayaking and canoeing but too shallow for the motorized boats. The shoreline ranges from sandy beaches to marsh. As the reservoir's water levels change, there are many areas that remain untouched.

It is possible to paddle year-round because temperatures do not dip below freezing except during the heart of winter. The canyon is typically several degrees cooler than nearby Ogden. So during the summer months it can be a nice repose from the heat.

I prefer to paddle in the early morning when there is still mist on the surface; the migratory birds are fishing, and most of the boaters are still sleeping while at anchor. At this time, the paddling is beautiful and quite often exclusive.

Pineview is not a remote getaway, but rather a well-accommodated and easily accessed location, which makes it well suited for those who want to intersperse some paddling with a camping trip or a quick day on the water.

CAUSEY RESERVOIR
County: Weber
LONG/LAT: N41 17.448 W111 34.988
Elevation: 5,698 feet/1,737 meters

Body Type: Reservoir

Difficulty: Easy to moderate. Canyon winds can make getting back a workout.

Season: Spring, summer, autumn

Size: 142 acres

Directions: From Ogden, take the 12th Street exit and head west up Ogden Canyon. Once in Ogden Valley, take the road following the south side of Pineview Reservoir. Take a right on UT 39. At Red Rock Ranch, take a right and continue until you get to Causey.

Put-in: At the top of the dam, you can head north or south. At the end of either road is a parking lot with an excellent place to launch. The south parking area has a bit longer portage, but is not muddy and marshy.

Other Sports: Fishing, camping, bird-watching, hiking, climbing, swimming

Information: www.recreation.gov/detail.cfm?ID=1172

Paddle Overview

If I were forced to select which reservoir is my favorite, I would pick Causey. The fact that it is very close to my home contributes a lot to this choice. However, Causey is also a wonderful place to paddle. Its massive cliffs, hidden coves, and beautiful scenery make it an ideal place for those living in the Wasatch Front Region.

Causey is unlike other paddle locations because it is very accessible, but has all the traits of the more remote waters. Immense cliffs stretch hundreds of feet in the air. At the base of the rock faces, you can find fascinating coves to navigate. In addition, the reservoir is broken down into five narrowing canyons that provide excellent cover and a very satisfying paddle.

Each narrow canyon has a small stream at the end that feeds Causey and the reservoir and river below it. The natural flows, where Cochone salmon spawn and trout congregate, provide excellent places to sit and listen to the trickle of the water.

Paddling along the base of one of the many rock faces of Causey

The true beauty of Causey is its suitability for paddling. It really is a paddler's paradise. With restrictions against powerboats, the worst you will see is an occasional trolling motor. In addition, because there are so many fun spots to explore and paddle, you can spend an entire day just slipping in and out of coves and corners.

If Causey has any faults, it is the wind coming through the canyons. On certain days, it can create some serious chop and make paddling tricky. Normally the winds blow moderately, and you head home feeling tired from all the enjoyment.

Scores of people have discovered the beautiful setting Causey provides. During the summer, and especially on weekends, you will find many other people on the water. From sea kayaks to aluminum canoes, every kind of boat is represented. Normally a crowd might get you down, but this feels more like a community of paddlers congregating to celebrate the joys of this sport.

Beyond paddling, you will find that Causey is a popular fishing and swimming spot. Many thrill seekers take to climbing the cliffs and jumping into the waters. Sadly, this results in injuries and even deaths every year. You will want to be careful when you enter the center finger of the reservoir.

Causey is not far away, but it feels remote. Once you are there, your soul and mind drift. Perhaps it is the cavernous cliffs or the icy green waters. Whatever it is, every summer I find myself at Causey, drawn to paddle again and again.

LOST CREEK RESERVOIR

County: Morgan
LONG/LAT: N41 11.070 W111 22.571
Elevation: 6,000 feet/1,829 meters
Body Type: Reservoir
Difficulty: Moderate
Season: Spring, summer, autumn
Size: 365 acres

Directions: From Ogden, take I-84 east to the Croydon exit. Croydon is located just past Morgan. Get off the exit and follow UT 158 north. The road is named Croydon Road, and it turns into Lost Creek Road. Follow it for 10 miles until you reach the dam.

Put-in: The ideal put-in is on the east side of the dam toward the end of the canyon. You will have to navigate around the canyon on a mixed dirt and paved road to get to the boat launch. The launch is fairly primitive, but there is parking and easy access to the water.

Other Sports: Fishing, camping

Information: www.recreation.gov/detail.cfm?ID=1191

Paddle Overview

The drive to Lost Creek brings to mind what its name conveys. You definitely feel lost. The long drive from the interstate seems to endlessly twist and turn through an empty valley, and just when you are considering turning around, you see the dam.

Lost Creek, 10 miles from the nearest civilization, is a good-sized reservoir and an interesting, complex paddle. The two lengthy canyons converge at the dam. The put-in places you near the end of one canyon, and thus, you have to paddle the entire length of the reservoir if you truly want to enjoy it.

The landscape surrounding the reservoir is sparse and reflects the high-desert climate of the region. Sagebrush and small juniper trees adorn the steep shoreline. You can also find cactus and other scrub plants here. However, this dry environment does not detract from the paddle experience.

In the northern canyon there is an island located where I have taken a small picnic. It is not the most exciting island, but I like it nonetheless. Also, with the steep canyon walls, the reservoir narrows toward the ends and keeps the paddling interesting.

Lost Creek is a state park. However, it has limited amenities compared to the other parks I have visited. In fact, on my visits I have never seen a ranger or park employee. In most cases, the place has been empty.

Happy and *lost* at Lost Creek Reservoir

On weekends, you may find a few people fishing, and I have been lucky enough to run into some other paddlers.

As with the other canyon paddles, you run the risk of getting windy conditions and choppy water. On the other hand, this is the only way you will get rough water. Motorized boats are prohibited at the reservoir. So if you have to get lost somewhere, Lost Creek is an ideal spot.

JORDAN RIVER
County: Utah, Salt Lake, Davis
LONG/LAT: N40 43.995 W111 55.402

Elevation: 4,209 feet/1,283 meters

Body Type: River

Difficulty: Moderate. Portages and obstacles add challenge to this normally docile river.

Season: Spring, summer, autumn, winter

Size: 58 miles

Directions: Depending on the spot you want to put in, directions can vary. I suggest planning a trip based on your location and then establish a put-in and take-out.

Put-in: There are numerous spots along the Jordan that are suitable to put in. I used the parking lot of Raging Waters at 1700 South and 1200 West. I suggest you visit the noted Web site before planning a visit.

Other Sports: Fishing, bird-watching

Information: www.parks-recreation.org/parks/html/jordan.html

Paddle Overview

The Jordan River is a fascinating place in the urban landscape that is the Salt Lake Valley. The Jordan connects the Wasatch Front and three counties. As it carves its way through farmland, neighborhoods, and industrial zones, the river transforms and evolves.

Unique in many ways, the Jordan is a northbound river. Traveling between Utah Lake and the Great Salt Lake, it is a river with a long history. Originally called the Utah River, the Mormons renamed it to evoke their pious heritage. Along its 58-mile trek, it is diverted, dammed, gated, and polluted.

The Jordan is not always a pleasant place, and often you need to be prepared to portage past some serious obstacles. However, it is a living river with the wildlife to prove it. As you paddle past roads, bridges, and other modern structures, you will note the vibrant life surrounding you. Beavers and muskrats swim. Birds nest. The entire place is teeming with life.

Enjoying a pleasant section of the Jordan River

The great thing about the Jordan is easy access, which permits you to paddle in the middle of an urban atmosphere. Take a lunch break, drop into the river, and paddle a few miles. You will be fascinated and maybe startled by the interesting paddle that exists in a city's backyard.

There are many organizations that are working hard to make a single continuous hiking, biking, and paddling trail along the Jordan. From the Utah County line in the south to the Davis County line in the north, this effort promotes cleanup and preservation of the river and its banks.

On my trip, I found the Jordan to be a truly delightful and surprisingly beautiful spot. The river has very little current, and I was able to tool around, paddle upstream, and play with little effort. I noted the river manages to continue to press forward while human "progress" tries to push it around.

Of course the Jordan did have some grimy areas. However, I would not be disheartened. In fact, consider taking a trash bag along and contributing to its cleanup. All told, the Jordan River is a diamond in the rough. With a little polish, she will certainly shine again.

LITTLE DELL RESERVOIR

County: Salt Lake
LONG/LAT: N40 47.335 W111 40.600
Elevation: 5,798 feet/1,767 meters
Body Type: Reservoir
Difficulty: Moderate. Constant winds make it a bit challenging.
Season: Spring, summer, autumn
Size: 249 acres
Directions: From Salt Lake, take I-80 east up Parley's Canyon. Take the East Canyon exit (#134) and then head northeast to the Little Dell Reservoir. The reservoir entrance is clearly marked and on the right.
Put-in: There is a small boat ramp on the west side of the reservoir. From the entrance, take a right and follow the road all the way down to the bottom.
Other Sports: Fishing, camping, bird-watching, hiking, climbing, swimming
Information: None

Paddle Overview

When it comes to paddling, there is something to be said about convenience. Often, the time it takes to get the gear and boat together consumes as much time as it takes to get to the water. Thus, when a destination is convenient and close to your home, you enjoy it all that much more. Little Dell is paddle of convenience.

Located just a quick drive up Emigration or Parley's Canyons, Little Dell is less than 20 minutes from downtown Salt Lake. Now just because it is close, does not mean it is some slipshod paddle. This large spot offers lovely mountain views and a delightful setting.

The green hills above the reservoir contrast nicely with the icy blue waters, and the inviting landscape beckons the paddler. The mountains, trees, and shores all combine to make this convenient location a nice reprieve from the urban landscape most endure on a daily basis.

Little Dell inhabits the bottom of a small valley. When you approach its cusp, you will note that you have to actually drive down to the water for the put-in. A short, twisting passage on the west side of the reservoir brings you to the water's edge. This is a terrific launch, and there is parking at the bottom, which can be a problem.

If it is a busy day, the small parking area by the boat ramp becomes filled, and you will have to go back to one of the two upper parking lots. Numerous trails carved in the side of the hill bring you back down, or you can just follow the road. This aspect of paddling at Little Dell can be inconvenient. You may have to leave all your gear on the shore while you hike back down to the launch.

On the water, conditions are usually a touch windy. The north end of the reservoir is much shallower and easier to paddle than when you get closer to the dam. At that end, the wind blows consistently, and it can be taxing to get a good clip going. While the wind is constant, it is not overwhelming.

The north end also has an area for picnicking and relaxing. The remainder of the reservoir has very little beach or accessible shoreline. Yet there is ample space to paddle, and that is the key. Little Dell is an oasis that provides a beautiful paddle with quick access from the Wasatch Front.

The road down into the convenient Little Dell Reservoir

WEBER RIVER

County: Weber
LONG/LAT: N41 10.028 W111 59.936
Elevation: 4,320 feet/1,317 meters
Body Type: River
Difficulty: Easy to moderate
Season: Spring, summer
Size: 4–5 miles
Directions: Heading north to Ogden, take the Riverdale Road exit. Follow Riverdale to West 700 South. Make a right and then an immediate left. Cross the bridge and continue to the end of the road and a parking lot. The take-out is located at Fort Buenaventura. Take the 24th Street exit and head east. Just before going over the viaduct, make a right and continue to the end of the road.
Put-in: Put in at Riverdale City Hall and river parkway and take out at Fort Buenaventura.
Other Sports: Fishing
Information: www.ogdencvb.org/fortb.html
www.riverdalecity.com/departments/recreation/trails.htm

Paddle Overview

The Weber is one of the grand rivers of Utah. It begins in the Unita Mountains, picks up the Ogden along the way, and flows into the Great Salt Lake. The river has many gentle spots and some decent rapids. However, the segment covered here is strictly an urban adventure.

There are a few things you need to know before deciding on this short but sweet trip. First, the water levels are going to be decent only in spring and early summer. Once the heat and irrigation begin to kick in, the water level drops too much to make it a worthwhile trip.

Next, the river remains shallow in spots throughout the year, and you may end up scratching your boat or getting stuck. However, simply get out and give yourself a little push, and you will be on your way again. Effective navigation can help you avoid some of these shallows.

Beginning in the Uintas, the Weber flows into the Great Salt Lake.

Last, there is a 2-foot-high constructed waterfall along the way. I was able to navigate my canoe over it with little trouble, but if you are concerned, you may want to portage around it. The water seemed somewhat deep after the falls, and thus, you do not need to worry about running aground.

If you are prepared for these hurdles, you are ready for a nice little adventure. Other than some foliage and bushes getting in the way, this is an excellent urban paddle. Much of the journey is calm water, though there are short periods with some tiny rapids. In all, there is nothing to fear.

The river is relatively slow and gentle after you put in at Riverdale. It is an easy spot to navigate; while the water moves at this spot, it is not overpowering. If you are concerned, the Greenway Trail covers a large area, and you can find a suitable place to launch.

Along the way, note the large number of birds that make their home along the shoreline. I saw amazing varieties on my journey and caught sight of a muskrat making its home in one of the small eddies.

Much of the area along the river is uninhabited. The paddle takes you by the train yards of the old Union Pacific and underneath a number of viaducts. You will see areas that appear to have been untouched for years and others that have some recent unclean visitors. In all, the paddle is certainly interesting and fun.

Taking out at Fort Buenaventura is also a breeze. This historic location was the first permanent settlement in the great basin. The tall shade trees and beautiful greenery make a perfect spot for a picnic after you have completed your trip.

This is a relatively short journey; while you may be encouraged to go farther, there are some more aggressive rapids ahead. Only those with an interest in whitewater should continue past the fort. Otherwise, this brief but beautiful paddle is great as a morning or half-day excursion.

OTHER DESTINATIONS

CURRANT CREEK RESERVOIR
County: Wasatch
LONG/LAT: N40 20.039 W111 03.041
Size: 500 acres
Directions: From Heber City, follow US 40 east for 30 miles. About 5 miles past Strawberry, turn left on a dirt road. Follow the dirt road for about 10 miles to the reservoir.

Comment: Currant Creek almost made the list as a Best Bet. However, be prepared for miles of bumpy and dusty road. In addition, the wind takes away a lot of the creek's appeal. It is a nice spot with a lot of pine trees and good camping.

DEER CREEK

County: Wasatch

LONG/LAT: N40 26.836 W111 28.709

Size: 3,260 acres

Directions: From Ogden, take I-84 east to the Morgan exit. Follow UT 66 south for 12 miles until you get to the reservoir.

Comment: Deer Creek is very popular with powerboaters and personal watercraft operators. On the south canyon, there is some moderately nice paddling, but you have to always keep your eye out for the errant motorized craft.

EAST CANYON

County: Morgan

LONG/LAT: N40 52.726 W111 34.906

Size: 680 acres

Directions: From Ogden, take I-84 east to the Morgan exit. Follow UT 66 south for 12 miles until you get to the reservoir.

Comment: Large, open, and popular with boaters, East Canyon has some admirable qualities. However, it is fairly featureless and not ideal for paddling. There are some nice spots on the south end of the reservoir near Big Rock if you choose to visit this state park.

JORDANELLE RESERVOIR

County: Wasatch

LONG/LAT: N40 52.726 W111 34.906

Size: 3,300 acres

Directions: From Salt Lake, take I-80 east to US 40 to UT 32. Then take the Rock Cliff exit.

Comment: The Jordanelle Reservoir is a very popular destination with the Salt Lake and Park City crowd. I prefer to go over to the opposite side of the reservoir near the Rock Cliff Nature Center. This beautiful little area on the Provo River is located in wetlands and is ideal for paddling. The state maintains a learning area for exploration of the wildlife on the river.

UTAH LAKE

County: Utah
LONG/LAT: N40 14.105 W111 44.208
Size: 96,600 acres
Directions: From Provo, take I-15 and exit at Provo Center Street. Go west on Center Street for 3 miles to the state park entrance.
Comment: Utah Lake is one that I leave to the powerboaters and sailboats. It is a big place, and while the state park is terrific, the view of the steel plant and the surrounding area is not. There are far prettier and more enjoyable places to paddle without the choppy water and dangerous conditions.

SOLDIER CREEK AND STRAWBERRY RESERVOIR

County: Wasatch
LONG/LAT: N40 10.987 W111 01.653
Size: 17,200 acres
Directions: From Heber City, follow US 40 east for 25 miles. You will note signs for Strawberry and Soldier Creek marinas. Both marinas have available put-ins and are a short drive from US 40.
Comment: Strawberry and Soldier Creek combine to make an exceptionally large reservoir noted for its excellent fishing. The Soldier Creek side is much better for paddling. The narrows and surrounding waters are more protected, and you can find many decent coves for shore paddling.

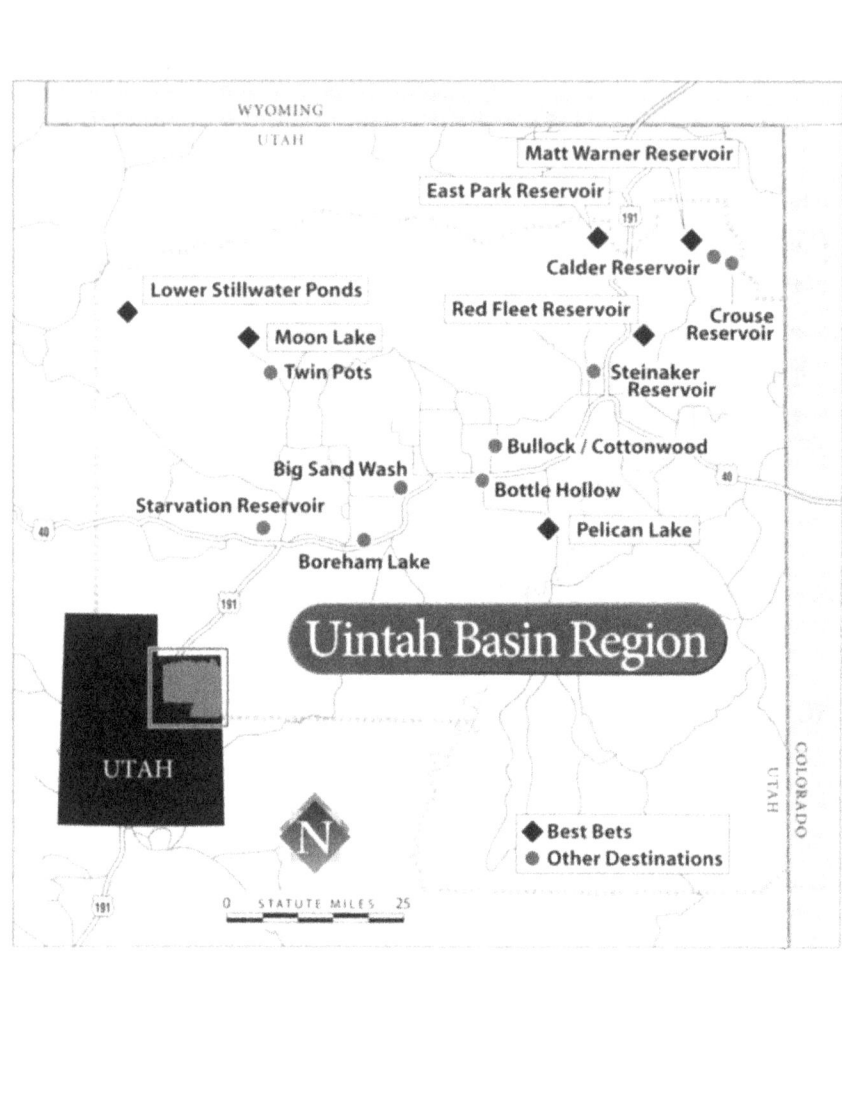

CHAPTER

5

The Uintah Basin is *not* a wasteland with miles of emptiness.

Uintah Basin Region

For years I had heard the Uintah Basin was a barren and destitute place. It was supposed to be a wasteland with miles of emptiness. However, through researching this book, I have discovered that this is completely inaccurate. In fact, the Uintah Basin is a gem filled with some of the best spots to paddle in the state and worth every mile of driving to visit.

Duchesne and Uintah counties have the benefit of sitting on the south slope of the Uinta Range. While the vast majority of the terrain is a massive plateau, it is also home to some of the most beautiful glacial lakes in the state. Sadly, many of these lakes are inaccessible by anything other than hiking. However, there are a few special destinations accessible by car, and they are noted in this section.

The largest portion of the basin is spread out and empty. You can expect to trek across a lot of open terrain to get from place to place, but the setting is beautiful and very interesting. One of the key industries of the Uintah Basin is oil. As you drive you will see the pumps swaying up and down as they harvest the fuel from the earth.

While the oil industry and farming are a big part of the economy, tourism has been steadily growing. Vernal has become the gateway to discovering dinosaurs in the state. You will find numerous dinosaur-themed exhibits, advertisements, and kitsch. A delightful little town, Vernal has embraced its dinosaur history.

Just west of Vernal is Dinosaur National Monument. This attraction is noted as one of the premier dinosaur-bone quarries in the world. Eleven different species of dinosaur have been found so far. There is a visitors center where you can watch paleontologists work on actual projects. This is a great place for kids and adults alike

Vernal, the largest population center in the region, is home to terrific restaurants and quaint shops—a virtual hub for recreation. In addition to all the paddling locations noted in this chapter, Flaming Gorge and the Ashley National Forest are to the north and west, and the Green River is to the east and south.

Duchesne (pronounced *doo-shane*) is a small rural community set close to the Uintah, Ouray, and Ute Native American tribal lands. Abraham Lincoln had the natives moved to the area from Provo in 1861 because of conflicts with Mormon settlers. To this day, the Native Americans own much of the county.

Fort Duchesne is the central location for tribal administration and offices. The tribe administrates three different bodies of water for paddling in the area; unlike the other waters in the area, these three require a boat permit acquired from the tribal office.

Duchesne County is by far the most lake-populated county in the state. Hundreds of lakes exist within its borders. However, most are not accessible and are rather petite. A drive on US 40 may make you think that this area is absent of water. Yet a short drive north, and you will find some of the most beautiful mountain spots in the West.

BEST BETS

MOON LAKE

County: Duchesne
LONG/LAT: N40 34.372 W110 30.539
Elevation: 7,573 feet/2,308 meters
Body Type: Lake
Difficulty: Moderate
Season: Summer only
Size: 768 acres
Directions: From Duchesne, take US 40 to UT 87 and head north for approximately 15 miles. The road bends and turns south. At the top of the hill, turn left. There is a sign indicating the turn to Moon Lake. Follow the road north until you come to the T intersection. Make a right and continue for about 15 miles to Moon Lake.
Put-in: Depending on the water level, much of the shore is available. A boat ramp is at the south end, but that end is not the most scenic part of the lake.
Other Sports: Fishing, camping, bird-watching, hiking
Information: www.moonlakeresort.com

Paddle Overview

There are certain things in nature that we equate with perfection. The designs of a snowflake, the majesty of a grand oak, the fluttering wings of a hummingbird—these things evoke amazement and respect. Moon

Paddling Moon Lake, a natural lake on the southern slopes of the Uintas

Lake, a natural lake surrounded by mountains and forest, could be one of those perfect things.

Moon Lake creates an epiphany in people who love to paddle. It retains all the elements that inspire joy in this sport. You approach the lake, realize how beautiful the paddling will be and how much fun you are going to have, and suddenly you are overcome with joy.

Moon is a natural lake located on the south slope of the Uintas. As you trek through the farmlands of rural Utah, you gain elevation and see a shift in the landscape. The forest becomes dense and fragrant as you climb into the valley. Arriving at the lake, you find tall pines and thickets of aspens all around and in the background, beautiful mountains.

Moon is a large lake but not overwhelming. Most paddlers can take on its length. The south end is not as attractive as the north. The scenery opens and flattens, and you reach a simple dam that helps keep the lake large. However, I found it a nice challenge to work my way southward and then return north with a view of the mountains in front of me.

The view is special because it is part of a canyon. The southern half has mountains on one side and the campground and lower hills to the west. As you paddle out, the Round Mountains enclose the area, and you have a gorgeous canyon paddle with steep shores, cascading waterfalls, and scenic coves to explore.

If Moon Lake has any problems, it is the fact that the lake is used for irrigation, so the shoreline gradually descends as the summer heat bears down on the region. The later in the season you arrive, the longer your portage will be. My visit was in late summer, and I had to carry the boat more than 100 yards to a mucky shore.

There is a wonderful trail that takes you around the lake and then climbs up to 10,000 feet. There are scenic mountain lakes on this trail as well and unless you are interested in carrying an inflatable or the portage of a lifetime, you may have to miss them as paddle experiences. Fish Creek feeds the lake throughout the year, and there is a popular trailhead on the east side of the lake.

Moon Lake has a terrific resort with cabins available to rent. The lodge is small and charming, and its numerous cabins are very quaint. Around since the 1920s, these little log dwellings are nothing fancy. However, they remind you that you came to the lake to spend some time outdoors.

The resort defines itself as rustic for a reason. The accommodations are not hotel quality, but rather simple rooms to clean fish and to throw off dirty paddling gear. The kind people at the resort told me that they think of the cabins as an improvement over a tent, but not by much.

The little store in the lodge has an excellent collection of all the necessities, including conveniently wrapped bundles of firewood. It also rents kayaks and canoes if you don't feel like dragging your boat to the lake. Everyone at the resort was friendly, charming, and funny.

One morning I got up just as the mist was burning off the water and paddled up into the canyon. The temperatures were brisk; the scenery was intoxicating. There was a light chop on the water, and yet my paddling felt effortless. I saw numerous industrious fishermen and got a kind morning wave.

This lake seems to bring out the best in everyone. I camped, and the gentleman in the site next to mine shared his delicious chili with me. My friend's son forgot to bring a sleeping bag, and the lodge loaned us one at no charge. Perhaps we got lucky, or perhaps being surrounded by perfection starts to rub off.

LOWER STILLWATER PONDS

County: Duchesne
LONG/LAT: N40 30.646 W110 34.950
Elevation: 7,410 feet/2,259 meters
Body Type: Lakes
Difficulty: Easy
Season: Spring, summer, autumn, winter
Size: Approximately 20 acres
Directions: From Duchesne, take US 40 to UT 87 and head north for approximately 15 miles. The road bends and turns south. At the top of the hill, turn left. Once in Mountain Home, take a left onto 6750 North and follow it up the canyon. There are signs noting Lower Stillwater.
Put-in: There is a river access area just off the road. Note the waypoint, and you will see the entrance.
Other Sports: Fishing, camping, bird-watching, hiking, climbing, swimming

The massive dam just above Lower Stillwater

Information: www.reserveusa.com/jsp/commonpage.jsp?goto=/nrrs/ut/yelp/newindex.html

Paddle Overview

When I went to visit this spot, I was initially looking forward to seeing Upper Stillwater. According to my maps, there was a huge reservoir with a massive canyon in a beautiful setting. What I found was a dam of amazing proportions and little paddling. However, as I descended the canyon in disappointment, I found a wonderful alternative worthy of a paddle.

Lower Stillwater was created when the dam changed the dynamics of the wetlands. Rock Creek remains below the dam; as part of the restoration of the region, large wetland areas have been created. These wetlands provide ponds and marsh to paddle.

There may not be as much here to paddle as other locations, but the destination has something unique. The whole area is a fascinating and alluring portion of a large river valley. The experience could be treated like a river paddle or a lake paddle. The open areas definitely feel like lake paddling. However, upstream there were enticing sections that make you think of a river trip.

The north part of this canyon is private property, and the south enters a Native American reservation. Thus, any river trip may be only 5 or 6 miles. Regardless, the ponds in the central section are part of public lands and open for paddling.

The water here is gentle and yielding with beautiful clarity. It is everything you could hope for in a paddle. There are soft islands of marshy grass to navigate around, and long, undulating pathways stretch north and south from the entrance. It is a genuinely lovely place.

These ponds are nicely placed in the middle of the valley. You will need to enter from the road and drive a short bit to get to the water's edge. There is not a lot of parking out near the ponds, and you may have to drop your gear and park back at the roadside lot if too many vehicles are blocking the route.

There are delightful sites at the nearby Yellowpine Campground, and access to the river is close by. This is a popular camping area because of the scenery. The ponds are exceptionally popular for fly-fishing. You will see people with waders casting as you travel up and down the canyon.

Upper Stillwater is not really suitable for paddling. On my visit, the water was so low that only a treacherous climb would have given me access to the water. However, the dam is impressive, and there are some terrific trails and campgrounds nearby.

You certainly can make the most of your trip to Lower Stillwater if you journey though the entire canyon. It is a fertile green river valley with stunning views, great campgrounds, and some charming paddling in the form of ponds.

PELICAN LAKE

County: Uintah
LONG/LAT: N40 10.932 W109 41.664
Elevation: 4,848 feet/1,478 meters
Body Type: Lake
Difficulty: Moderate
Season: Spring, summer, autumn
Size: 1,680 acres
Directions: From Vernal, head west on US 40. Take a left on UT 88. At the bottom of the hill, follow the road to the right when you see the reservoir. Follow the signs. The road takes you to the west and then south side of the reservoir. It starts paved and then turns to a graded gravel road.
Put-in: There is a good boat ramp with a pier on the south side of the lake.
Other Sports: Fishing, camping, bird-watching
Information: www.recreation.gov/detail.cfm?ID=2142

Paddle Overview

On your approach to Pelican's shores, you come off a large plateau and descend down a steep drive. Suddenly, among all the brown and tan, there is the beautiful blue pool. There are few places that can actually be defined as a true oasis. Most times, the word is a euphemism for a healthy spot in a troubled environment. Yet Pelican Lake is an oasis and so much more.

Just north and west of the curving Green River, Pelican Lake is a place that defies description. On the south side, you have fields of stark sagebrush where prairie dogs and rattlesnakes are at home. On the north, you have this deep plateau that quickly descends and rises. Like a natural limbo, there is Pelican.

This moderate-sized natural lake beckons to be paddled. Unlike its cousins closer to the mountains, Pelican has few trees or defining landscape; however, its large marshes and stunning blue color make it an attractive spot. Paddlers will find a lot to explore and even more to enjoy.

An oasis, Pelican Lake

Because of its size and the scarcity of water in the region, Pelican is also a favorite among shorebirds looking to take break and get a bite to eat. If you do not have an interest in watching pelicans, bald eagles, or cranes, pack your fishing pole.

Pelican Lake is known for its fishing, specifically bluegill. Many champion-sized fish have been caught here. In addition, the lake is stocked with bass. Because of this, you will find people shore fishing and out in small fishing craft trying to land the big one.

There is camping at the lake and some small tree coverage near its shore. However, a vast majority of the area is very exposed. The sky seems endless when you are on the water. For someone who is normally used to seeing mountains, the experience is refreshing and interesting.

Pelican is a good paddle spot. The marshy shoreline and tall grasses make it a scenic yet subtle place to explore. This delicate wetland inside the Uintah Basin does not seem like it belongs where it sits, but perhaps that is what truly defines an oasis.

RED FLEET RESERVOIR

County: Uintah
LONG/LAT: N40 35.129 W109 26.526
Elevation: 5,735 feet/1,748 meters
Body Type: Reservoir
Difficulty: Moderate
Season: Spring, summer, autumn
Size: 520 acres
Directions: From Vernal, head north on US 191 for about 13 miles. The reservoir entrance is on the right, and you can't see it until you come to the state park entrance.
Put-in: There is a marina with a boat ramp just inside the state park entrance.
Other Sports: Fishing, camping, hiking, climbing, swimming
Information: www.recreation.gov/detail.cfm?ID=1195

Paddle Overview

You will note that several of the state parks in this book have been overlooked for paddling. For the most part, I avoid these locations because of boat traffic, crowds, and generally choppy water conditions. You see, I enjoy paddling because I want a serene and personal experience. The state parks lure people from across Utah to recreate, and as such, they are not ideal.

Red Fleet Reservoir is an exception to the rule. This large reservoir north of Vernal is such a unique and fascinating destination that enduring crowds and powerboats is worthwhile for the opportunity to explore its smooth red sandstone cliffs and canyons walls.

Red Fleet is in the center of dinosaur country, and as you travel to it, you will note the numerous signs identifying the geological history tied to the formations. The ride is not only fascinating, but also educational. The signs note things like DINOSAURS ROAMED HERE or ANCIENT SEA BED.

Once you enter Red Fleet, you will immediately understand the reasons to endure crowds. The formations jutting from the water are fascinating and enticing. Unlike other destinations, the rock formations at this location are more important than the water. They are central to the experience of paddling here.

Part of the joy of paddling in a place like this is getting out of your boat and exploring some of the rocks. On the opposite side of the reservoir, there is the Dinosaur Trackway. This recently discovered attraction allows you to view actual dinosaur footprints believed to be more than 200 million years old.

The tracks have been preserved in sandstone and can be reached by hiking a trail filled with various uphill and downhill climbs. Many of these trails are close to the shore and can be found with a short search. The hike is a couple of miles; however, according to many, the best spot to view the tracks is on the rocks close to shore.

Red Fleet's colorful cliffs are slickrock and Navajo sandstone. They are smooth on your feet and a lot of fun to climb and investigate. However, be careful where you tread lest you damage the rocks or yourself. There are snakes and other dangerous animals in these wild areas.

Other attractive aspects of paddling Red Fleet are the numerous landscape and water features to explore. In certain areas there are abundant peninsulas, canyons, and channels to paddle around. Yet Red Fleet is a large place, and there are open spaces where powerboats will congregate.

Red Fleet is a desert lake, so you can expect warm water and soaring temperatures during the summer months. The rock seems to capture the heat and radiate it like an oven. There is little shade, so extra caution should be exhibited during the summer.

The colorful slickrock and Navajo sandstone of Red Fleet Reservoir

Your visit to Red Fleet can be educational, exciting, and interesting. You can experience the strong legacy of the dinosaurs and the mark they left on our earth both literally and figuratively all around Red Fleet.

MATT WARNER RESERVOIR
County: Uintah
LONG/LAT: N40 46.612 W109 18.235
Elevation: 7,659 feet/2,334 meters
Body Type: Reservoir

Matt Warner Reservoir is located in a hidden valley on the southeastern slope of the Uintas.

Difficulty: Moderate. Windy conditions make it a tougher paddle.

Season: Spring, summer, autumn

Size: 297 acres

Directions: From Vernal, take US 191 north about 20 miles to Limestone Road. From here you are on dirt. Take a right and continue east for about 12 miles. Take a left onto Jackson Draw Road, and follow it for about 1 mile. Take a right onto Lane County Road.

Put-in: There is a nice boat ramp on the south side of the reservoir. I would avoid a shore put-in because the land is quite marshy. Also, there is a fence around most of the reservoir.

Other Sports: Fishing, camping
Information: None

Paddle Overview

As you approach Matt Warner Reservoir, you see fields and rolling hills. It is not a very prominent spot or noticeable at first, but as you get closer, you start to understand what is attractive about this destination. This is a hidden valley that holds a special place to paddle.

Matt Warner is located on the southeastern slope of the Uinta Range, where the mountains drop in elevation and begin to spread out. Wide open space is spread between the smaller peaks. It is a windswept, quiet place, and there are miles of dirt road to cover before you arrive at the water.

One thing that comes to mind when you approach the reservoir is how natural the setting seems to be. Many times, the reservoirs of Utah seem out of place. They appear to be formed or forced. Matt Warner is the opposite. Its location molds and forms to the valley floor, and the surrounding mountains look as if they are holding it in their hands.

The reservoir is named after a noted outlaw who hung out with Butch Cassidy and committed a series of bank robberies. Warner was wiser than most and retired from crime to settle in Utah. However, on a prospecting trip he was ambushed, and he killed two men. He was sent to prison for the crime, but later returned to become a justice of the peace, a deputy sheriff, and a detective in Price, Utah.

The feeling of the Old West permeates the area. Located on Diamond Mountain Plateau, this area brings to life the open range and cowboys driving cattle.

The reservoir is round and fenced around its shore. The confines hold large marshy wetlands that normally might be difficult to access. However, the south side has a boat ramp, rest rooms, and parking. In addition, facilities exist on the north side, but there is a steeper drop to the shore.

The paddling can get a bit choppy as the wind brushes the water's surface. Matt Warner's orientation and smooth embankments provide a little protection from the wind, but the reservoir is large enough that the wind is a valid concern for novice paddlers. You may have to contend with some strong winds and work hard to get back to your put-in.

The winds may also be an issue when camping. While campsites are available, the highly exposed plateau may make your stay windy and uncomfortable. You may consider looking for a spot several miles up the west canyon or closer to the mountains on the south.

Yet this spot is definitely beautiful and interesting. Something about Matt Warner speaks to me. Perhaps it is the smooth lines of the landscape, the sentimental Western atmosphere, or my simple love of paddling gentle water. I am not certain what the attraction is, but I know I will return.

EAST PARK RESERVOIR

County: Uintah
LONG/LAT: N40 46.802 W109 33.141
Elevation: 8,999 feet/2,743 meters
Body Type: Lake
Difficulty: Moderate
Season: Spring, summer, autumn
Size: 132 acres
Directions: From Vernal, head north on US 191 for about 22 miles. Turn west on Forest Service Road 018. There are signs to East Park at this intersection. Follow this road for about 7 miles to a fork. Follow the right fork for the final mile to the reservoir. If you continue on the left fork about 1 mile, there is a great scenic view above the reservoir off a road on the right.
Put-in: There is good shore access from the south side.
Other Sports: Fishing, camping, bird-watching
Information: None

Towering pines on the shores of East Park Reservoir

Paddle Overview

It is amazing that you pass the white plateau shores of Steinaker Reservoir and the Navajo sandstone of Red Fleet Reservoir before arriving at East Park Lake Reservoir. There are very few regions in the state where you can experience such geologically diverse paddles within an hour of driving. Yet completing this paddling trifecta is not only possible, but also easy.

East Park provides all the benefits of its sister lakes in the High Uintas. Beautiful mountain scenery, towering pines, and stunning views combine to make an idyllic paddling location. However, the aspect of East Park that really shines is its convenient location.

Rather than bumping along miles of dirt road, you reach East Park by taking a nicely paved road directly off US 191. The simple jaunt will take you past some campsites and through a field directly to the lake's shores. In addition, there is ample parking and a very easy portage.

For the most part, the winding road to East Park is a simple drive. It is well paved and nicely marked. However, it is a touch steep at points, and the curves that climb the mountain can be daunting. Regardless, even taking it slow will still require less than an hour.

This area of Utah is lumber country, and logging vehicles make their way up and down the road to East Park throughout the summer. However, there is little evidence of the logging near the reservoir. Trees are everywhere. The forest is dense and aromatic.

As a paddle, East Park is very pleasant. The surface is somewhat exposed; while the weather was perfect on my visit, I could sense a distinct wind. The flat area surrounding the lake combined with the reservoir's long form and an opening on either end appears to create a potential wind risk.

While the lake is not huge, it has a decent-sized surface area. It appears to be shallow near its shores with quickly increasing depth. This means you will experience significant variation in paddle experiences depending on your visit. There is a little more shore to trek across in late summer, and it can be a touch mucky. Nonetheless, this is not a sufficient enough issue to deter you from paddling.

East Park, Steinaker, and Red Fleet are three very different reservoirs in close proximity to one another. On a single visit to Vernal, you can get three different flavors of what this region has to offer. Not since a banana split has there been such a tempting offer.

OTHER DESTINATIONS

BIG SAND WASH
County: Duchesne
LONG/LAT: N40 17.123 W110 13.211
Size: 650 acres (2007)

Directions: From Duchesne, head east toward Roosevelt. US 40 takes a short turn to the north at Myton. Just as it begins to make its turn eastward again, make a left onto UT 87. Stay on UT 87 westbound until the reservoir takes a turn to the north. Big Sand Wash will be on your right.

Comment: My attempts to visit and paddle this fascinating location were thwarted by the fact that it had no water. Big Sand Wash is undergoing an improvement that will make it larger and more usable in the future. In speaking with the Central Utah Water District, I learned they plan to make a significant increase in the size. In fact, they are practically doubling the surface area to 650 acres. However, the project is not expected to be completed until the end of 2007.

BOREHAM LAKE (MIDVIEW RESERVOIR)
County: Duchesne
LONG/LAT: N40 10.543 W110 10.468
Size: 75 acres

Directions: About 12 miles east of Duchesne or 12 miles west of Myton, travel on US 40 and turn northwest. Go about 1 mile to Bridgeland. From Bridgeland, head northeast about 1.5 miles to a set of forks in the road. Keep right at the first two forks, then turn right on a road going east. Go about 2 miles to the reservoir.

Comment: This smaller reservoir is owned by the Ute Nation and requires a boat permit to be paddled. The tribal offices in Fort Duchesne can assist you if you choose to paddle this little lake. The setting is very rural and pretty, but the lake is not too large.

BOTTLE HOLLOW

County: Uintah

LONG/LAT: N40 10.543 W110 10.468

Size: 420 acres

Directions: You will find Bottle Hollow located just east of Roosevelt, right off US 40 in Fort Duchesne, next to the tribal offices.

Comment: You will be required to obtain a special boat permit to use this reservoir, which is located on the Ute Nation property. It is not an especially attractive location, although notes indicate that the fishing is fairly good. Its large size is appealing, but there are more scenic locations nearby.

BULLOCK LAKE AND COTTONWOOD LAKE

County: Uintah

LONG/LAT: Bullock N40 21.151 W109 49.158
Cottonwood N40 21.218 W109 47.738

Size: Bullock approximately 10 acres
Cottonwood approximately 30 acres

Directions: From Vernal, head west on US 40. Take a right just past Gusher on 9500 East. Follow the road north for a couple of miles. On the right there is a small dirt road that takes you directly to the reservoir.

Comment: These two small lakes are located next to one another. The red rock setting is very nice and quaint. Both lakes are a bit small and lack any real challenge, but have some fun features. Bullock has a small island in its center, and Cottonwood features a few cliffs along its otherwise bland shore.

CALDER RESERVOIR

County: Uintah

LONG/LAT: N40 43.788 W109 12.952

Size: Approximately 99 acres

Directions: From Vernal, take US 191 north about 20 miles to Limestone Road. From here you are on dirt. Take a right and continue east for about 12 miles. Take a left onto Jackson Draw Road, and follow it for about 1 mile. Take a right onto Lane County Road. Follow it past Matt Warner, staying to the right. The reservoir is on the left.

Comment: Reminiscent of the Old West and located east of Matt Warner, this small reservoir is surrounded by interesting rocks and hills. Its size is part of the charm that makes it worth a visit. If you want a small spot to be alone, Calder might be a good choice.

CROUSE RESERVOIR

County: Uintah
LONG/LAT: N40 43.574 W109 11.223
Size: Approximately 80 acres
Directions: From Vernal, take US 191 north about 20 miles to Limestone Road. From here you are on dirt. Take a right and continue east for about 12 miles. Take a left onto Jackson Draw Road and follow it for about 1 mile. Take a right onto Lane County Road. Continue past Matt Warner and Calder reservoirs. Follow the road as it goes to the right and continues around the reservoir.

Comment: Crouse is a touch smaller than its closest neighbor, Calder, but it is not very big. The landscape in this part of the Uintas is quite distinct, and Crouse is unique. However, it is a lot of dirt road for a relatively small paddle.

STARVATION RESERVOIR

County: Duchesne
LONG/LAT: N40 10.414 W110 29.509
Size: 3,495 acres
Directions: The reservoir is just east of Duchesne, directly off US 40. The area has excellent signs.

Comment: Extensive and open, Starvation is a hugely popular water-skiing spot just east of Duchesne. While it is large and frequented by powerboats, there are many small fingers to explore, and a paddler could make an interesting adventure checking out these areas.

STEINAKER RESERVOIR
County: Uintah
LONG/LAT: N40 30.959 W109 31.509
Size: 800 acres
Directions: The reservoir is just north of Vernal, directly off US 191. The area has excellent signs and is exceptionally easy to find.
Comment: Steinaker's plateau scenery and state-park services make it a popular spot with the locals. Hence, it is not an ideal location for paddlers. Much of the reservoir is open water and difficult to paddle on busy days. However, it is convenient to Vernal.

TWIN POTS
County: Duchesne
LONG/LAT: N39 20.712 W110 56.425
Size: Approximately 40 acres
Directions: From Duchesne, take US 40 to UT 87 and head north for approximately 15 miles. The road bends and turns south. At the top of the hill, turn left. There is a sign indicating the turn to Moon Lake. Follow the road north until you come to the T-intersection. Make a right and follow the road to Moon Lake for about 15 miles. Twin Pots are about halfway there on your left.
Comment: Located on Ute Nation property, these tandem lakes require a special boat permit from the tribal office in Fort Duchesne. The two lakes join in the center, and they are charming and have some nice features. However, you are almost to Moon Lake, why stop?

CHAPTER 6

The Uinta Range, the highest mountain range in the state

Uinta Range Region

The Uinta Range is geologically unique. It is the highest mountain range in the state and the only range to go from east to west in the lower 48 states. Elevations start around 7,000 feet in the lower valleys and climb to 13,528 feet at the top of Kings Peak, Utah's highest mountain.

This drastic change in altitude makes these mountains a dramatic back drop. Often, you can travel across miles of flat plain with mountain peaks following you in the distance. Throughout the year, these beautiful peaks remain snow-capped and stunning.

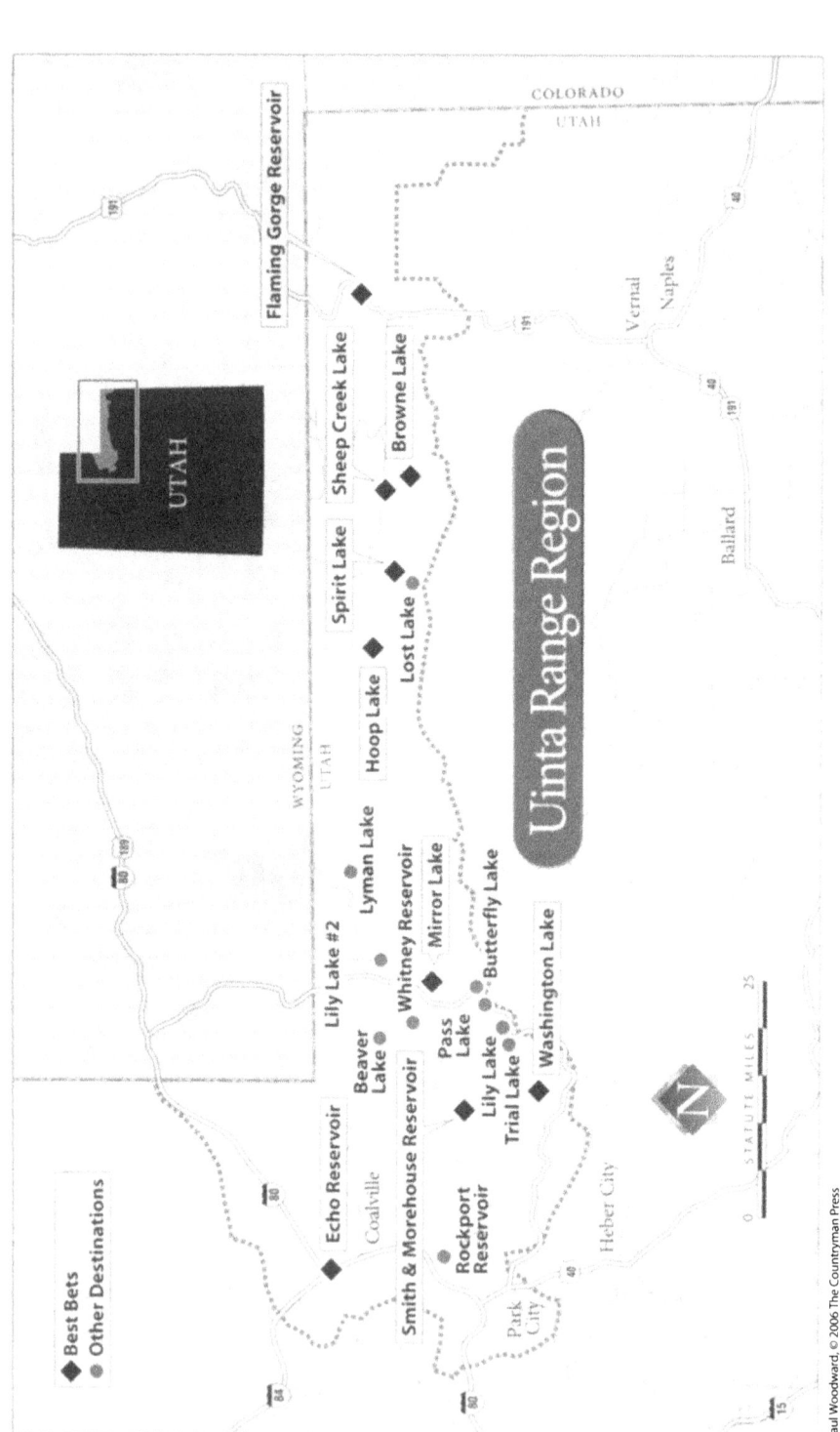

The high Uinta Range is home to moose, elk, and deer. It is not surprising to see all three on a visit. A glance upward will reveal numerous birds of prey. Bald eagles, hawks, and ospreys circle the area, hunting and fishing. Getting back to nature is a simple step when visiting this majestic range.

The difficulty with this region is that you can't always get from here to there. When looking at maps and seeing the illustrations, things appear easy and accessible. However, as you attempt to get to various spots, the roads are not what you might expect. Many times you may be confronted with rutted and rocky pathways.

If you choose to venture forth on anything in this region that is noted as a dirt road, consult the park-service rangers on the condition of the route. More than likely, they will have information or have been up on the road and visited the location. Winter avalanches, spring mudslides, and summer forest fires can change the accessibility of a road. Yet maps do not have this information.

Around this region, you will also notice there is little of what we commonly call civilization. There are few convenience stores, markets, or gas stations. These places are uncommon and often inaccessible any time other than summer. However, there are many small towns that sit just outside the entrance to the areas. Be certain to fuel up before venturing up.

Coalville is an appealing little town and the county seat of Summit County. It has a fun general store and a small but nice downtown. There are service stations and other facilities in town. You may or may not pass the city on your way to the Unitas, depending on your route.

The Flaming Gorge area is a very popular summer vacation spot. There are abundant locations to camp and stay. Services and a great lodge are available nearby in the small town of Dutch John. The town is close to the gorge and makes a great jumping off point for paddling many of the other waters in the region.

Manila, located just inside the Utah border with Wyoming, is the county seat for Daggett and is on the opposite side of Flaming Gorge. This tiny town, at the entrance of the Ashley National Forest, is open for business during the summer months because people use it as a route to get to the north slopes of the Uinta Range. It is a place that you might miss if you blink. However, it is one of the few service locations before heading up to the mountains.

Kamas, on the southwest side, is known as the gateway to the Uinta Range for a reason. This quaint little town is the supply post that most people visit before they head up the Mirror Lake Highway. You will find more-than-adequate businesses from which to get gas, ice, firewood, and some groceries. There are also fishing outfitters and spots to pick up paddle supplies.

Summit County's most prominent town is Park City. This resort area is famous for its main street with plentiful restaurants, shops, and bars. Park City is a year-round recreation destination. Mountain biking, hiking, and other activities abound during the summer and skiing, snowboarding, and Nordic skiing abound in the winter.

Park City was central to the 2002 Olympic Winter Games. Close to town is the Olympic Park, which allows people to experience the thrill of ski jumping, luge, and skeleton racing. No matter what time of year you visit, you can experience the thrill of the Olympic competition.

Park City, with all its grandeur, is quite far from most of the paddle destinations noted in this region. It is an excellent tourist destination, and many paddlers may make it a starting spot to explore the region. However, there are much closer locations.

The Uinta Range holds some of the most beautiful paddle spots in this book. The high-alpine scenery is a stunning setting for a paddle. Because the range is fairly convenient to the major metropolitan areas, you can experience many of these paddles within a couple hours of driving.

BEST BETS

THE MIRROR LAKE HIGHWAY

Running 78 miles from Kamas to Evanston, Wyoming, UT 150, also known as the Mirror Lake Scenic Byway, is a virtual paradise for pad-

Mirror Lake, one of the most popular destinations along the Mirror Lake Highway

dling. This route is decorated with numerous lakes in varying sizes and shapes. Each is beautiful, unique, and located in an absolute perfect setting.

Many are right along the highway and can be accessed by simply pulling over and putting in. There are also many lakes that are not accessible or require miles of dirt driving to access. However, UT 150 is well maintained, easy to drive, and provides excellent access to the lakes noted.

While I certainly had the desire to visit every lake in the region, I simply did not have the time or the resources to get to them all. I have focused my attention on those that can be easily accessed and that I believe provide a great paddle experience. However, I encourage anyone visiting this region to explore the entire area surrounding Mirror Lake.

Each lake has its own characteristics and interesting features. However, most are lined with pines and have stunning mountain views. In addition, the entire highway has excellent parking, rest rooms, and services. To me, the best paddles are Mirror (if the crowds are quiet) and Washington (because of its size). However, even the tiny little lakes like Teapot or Lily are worth a visit.

MIRROR LAKE

County: Duchesne
LONG/LAT: N40 42.611 W110 53.621
Elevation: 10,000 feet/3,048 meters
Body Type: Lake
Difficulty: Easy
Season: Summer
Size: 50 acres
Directions: From Kamas, Mirror Lake is located on UT 150. It is clearly marked and easy to find.
Put-in: At the end of the parking lot, there is a short but simple launch.
Other Sports: Fishing, camping, bird-watching, hiking, climbing
Information: www.utah.com/byways/mirror_lake.htm

Paddle Overview

Named Mirror for its incredible reflective surface and the stunning scenery you can view in the reflection, it is probably the most popular spot along the highway. The large parking lot and well-accommodated site are good indicators of the number of visitors who stop to hike, fish, and paddle around this scenic mountain lake.

On your approach to Mirror from the highway, you will see a dramatic overlook of the lake. From this vantage point, you can understand

Enjoying the reflections on Mirror Lake with Bald Mountain as a backdrop

why the road was given its name. None of the other bodies of water on the highway have quite the same view or the same impact.

Mirror is a grand paddle. It is small, but you feel like someone has dropped you in a little spot of heaven. The massive peak of Bald Mountain and the abundant trees are idyllic and invigorating. The whole experience would be perfect if it weren't for the crowds.

If you have to select one lake on the highway to paddle, Mirror is a good choice but not the best. Because of its popularity, you may have to contend with numerous other boaters. While powerboats are not allowed, that does not mean that the water can't get busy. However, Mirror is certainly a worthwhile visit. The picture-perfect setting and the dramatic approach will have your heart racing and your adrenaline pumping to get on the water.

WASHINGTON LAKE

County: Summit
LONG/LAT: N40 40.814 W110 57.683
Elevation: 9,992 feet/3,024 meters
Body Type: Lake
Difficulty: Easy
Season: Summer
Size: 94 acres
Directions: From Kamas, Washington Lake is located on UT 150. Washington and Trial Lakes are the first you approach. They are on the west side of the road. Turn left at the Trial Lake turnoff, turn left again after about 0.25 mile, and follow the road for about 0.5 mile. The lake is clearly marked and easy to find.
Put-in: On the campsite loop road there are numerous spots where you can drop your boat in the water.
Other Sports: Fishing, camping, bird-watching, hiking, climbing
Information: www.utah.com/byways/mirror_lake.htm

Paddle Overview

Washington is one of the largest of the destinations on the Mirror Lake Highway. It is almost double the size of Mirror and provides a lot of beautiful paddling areas to explore. The long shape and tree-lined shore make for a nice day on the water.

There is also a nice trail that surrounds the lake. Because of the easy shore access, you can pop off for a break and a nice hike, only to pop back in your boat and explore some more.

Washington Lake, the largest lake on the Mirror Lake Highway

The true beauty of Washington Lake is its campsites. There are numerous spots located directly next to the water. The shore rolls right up to the edge of many of the sites, and other sites are just across the way. You can plan on that early morning paddle just after rolling out of your sleeping bag.

Close to Washington is Trial Lake. It is a nice spot, but because of its close proximity to the road, it gets a lot more traffic. In addition, Trial is much smaller than Washington. However, it adds another dimension to a paddle trip.

Washington feels like it is a bit exposed. The south end is wide open. However, water conditions at the lake have been perfect on every visit I have made. Some hazards exist. There is a mixed shore with some rocky areas and felled trees. You need to keep a close eye on where you decide to stop because water levels shift.

Washington is a grand spot, worthy of its namesake. It is the first lake you will encounter coming from Kamas. It is first in size when compared to the other paddles along the highway and the first spot you will want to visit on your trip to the Uintas.

THE SPIRIT LAKE SCENIC BYWAY

Unlike the Mirror Lake Highway, the scenic route to Spirit Lake is not well paved, and there aren't as many lakes on it. However, these spots are still worthy of the drive if you have a decent vehicle and don't mind a little bit of rough road.

Located on the north slope of the Uintas, the Spirit Lake trek is a bit rougher on you. However, the payoff is excellent. The lakes of this region are mostly larger than those on the Mirror Lake Highway and many have much better camping spots.

The landscape here is much different. The slopes are less majestic, but more gentle. They lack the drama, and the views feel more relaxed and less accessible. The Spirit Lake byway is for those who want to really get away when they go for a paddle.

SPIRIT LAKE

County: Daggett
LONG/LAT: N40 50.246 W110 00.178
Elevation: 10,159 feet/3,096 meters
Body Type: Lake
Difficulty: Easy
Season: Summer
Size: 54 acres
Directions: From Manila, take UT 44 south to the Spirit Lake Scenic Byway. The byway entrance is just past Dowd's Hole to your right. The initial part of the journey is on paved road, but ends up on dirt. Follow the road and the signs 21 miles to Spirit Lake.

The not-so-rustic lodging at Spirit Lake

Put-in: There is a boat dock at the Spirit Lake Lodge. In addition, there is some easy-access shoreline from the campgrounds.
Other Sports: Fishing, camping, bird-watching, hiking
Information: 435-789-1181

Paddle Overview
Spirit Lake reminds me of something from the movies. The mountain lodge nestled against a stunning lake, surrounded by pines and wildlife is something our imaginations can easily create. However, there is nothing imaginary about this picture-perfect spot on the north slope of the Uintas.

Spirit Lake has earned the right to have the scenic byway named after it. The location has all the elements of a great paddle spot. What it does not have in size, it makes up in character. The soft marshy shoreline and stunning mountain views are the perfect compliment to the pastoral atmosphere of the place.

Spirit is very well protected from the elements. Trees and mountains surround this natural lake and make it a comfortable paddle. The shoreline has a few rocky spots and some sandy beaches. However, most of it is inaccessible.

The lodge at Spirit is a great family getaway. Small rustic cabins are placed sporadically around the property. They are charming little places with porches, fire pits, and warm interiors. Activities include horseback riding, volleyball, hiking, fishing, and of course, paddling.

There is a main lodge, which not only has a restaurant but also hosts entertainment and activities. The resort is very popular; if you are interested in visiting and staying, you should plan ahead and book early. The owner said that midweek is easier to book, so if you want a weekend escape, think ahead.

If you choose to camp, the drive to Spirit is one of the highlights of a visit. The long, straight dirt road is decorated with fantastic spots in wonderful settings. A small stream with large green areas and tall pines is just off the road, and there are abundant locations to pitch your tent.

BROWNE LAKE

County: Daggett
LONG/LAT: N40 51.652 W109 48.697
Elevation: 8,276 feet/2,523 meters
Body Type: Lake
Difficulty: Easy
Season: Summer
Size: 54 acres
Directions: From Manila, take UT 44 south to the Spirit Lake Scenic Byway. The byway entrance is just past Dowd's Hole to your right.

Browne, a quaint lake on the Spirit Lake Scenic Byway

The initial part of the journey is on paved road but ends up on dirt. The lake road is located about 3 to 4 miles on the left. There is a sign on the road, and the lake is about 0.5 mile away over a small hill.

Put-in: Depending on the water level, much of the shore is available. There is a short portage from the parking lot to the water, but nothing too difficult.

Other Sports: Fishing, camping, bird-watching, hiking

Information: 435-789-1181

Paddle Overview

Because the lake is nestled among some small hills, you approach the water with no suspicions of what lies beyond. You soon discover a quaint little lake located on the Spirit Lake Scenic Byway. This charming spot provides paddlers with a small but comfortable setting to explore, fish, and watch wildlife.

Pronounced *brownie*, this is a little spot with a simple formation. A large dam has been built to hold the water, and the lake's smooth shore makes it easy to take a quick paddle. While there are not a lot of trees, the hills surrounding the lake provide good protection from the wind and make Browne a nice place to stop.

Browne has specific benefits over other locations—it is quick and easy to find and has some nice camping along its shore. The short rolling hills and sparse tree coverage provide for places to stay. However, they also mean you have some exposure to the elements.

There are excellent facilities and ample parking at the lake. You can put in just off the dam or near the shore by some of the campsites. In either spot, you will find it convenient to get your boat in the water. Though the shoreline is marshy in some areas, you can find a dry spot to get into the water.

In all, I like Browne because it is conveniently located on the way to Spirit Lake. It is not as scenic as many other spots in the area, but remains a nice choice. You can take a little break and make camp with little effort. Choose Browne for its quaint charm and decent size.

HOOP LAKE

County: Summit
LONG/LAT: N40 54.383 W110 03.616
Elevation: 9,377 feet/2,858 meters
Body Type: Lake
Difficulty: Easy
Season: Summer
Size: 185 acres
Directions: From Manila, take UT 44 south to the Spirit Lake Scenic Byway. The byway entrance is just past Dowd's Hole to your right. The initial part of the journey is on paved road but ends up on

The dirt road driving to Hoop Lake is worth the effort.

dirt. The lake is located west about 25 miles on the left. Keep on the dirt road and be careful not to follow UT 221 as it heads north.

Put-in: Just over the dam there are a variety of shore spots suitable for a put-in.

Other Sports: Fishing, camping, bird-watching, hiking, climbing, swimming

Information: 435-789-1181

Paddle Overview

I was beat when we arrived at Hoop Lake. We had driven miles of dirt road, and my fingers were shaking from the washboard and constant rocks. However, the drive was well worth the effort. Hoop Lake is a delightful spot in the Uinta Range.

Hoop is a glacial lake with lovely scenery and easy access. It has a decent-sized surface area, and a large dam keeps water at good levels throughout the summer months. The shoreline is mostly sandy with easy access, and yet there are a large number of trees to provide decent protection from the wind.

I noted a number of great places to put-in, and you can easily paddle and then pull off for a picnic at one of the nice shore spots. I especially liked the large number of tall pines that sit a few yards from the shore. The only area lacking trees is by the dam.

This dense forest prevents you from viewing many of the peaks of the Uinta Range. However, the trees embrace you, and you can smell the aroma of pine while out on the water.

Hoop is not especially different than many of the lakes that are located on the northeastern slope of the Uintas, but it is excellent if you are looking for a tree-lined paddle experience. You also might appreciate Hoop's distance from other bodies of water and relatively simple layout.

SHEEP CREEK LAKE

County: Daggett
LONG/LAT: N40 53.276 W109 50.980
Elevation: 8,624 feet/2,629 meters
Body Type: Lake
Difficulty: Easy
Season: Summer
Size: 86 acres
Directions: From Manila, take UT 44 south to the Spirit Lake Scenic Byway. The byway entrance is just past Dowd's Hole to your right. The initial part of the journey is on paved road but ends up on dirt. The road to the lake is located about 5 miles on the right. There is a small sign on the road, and the lake is about 0.5 mile away.

Pines line the shore at Sheep Creek Lake.

Put-in: There is no boat ramp. The best location seems to be on the south side, near the Beaver Creek source. However, there is a lot of available shoreline from which to put in.

Other Sports: Fishing, camping

Information: www.go-utah.com/sheep-creek-spirit-lake-loop

Paddle Overview

When I first discovered Sheep Creek, I had already driven by it once. You see, it was not listed on my map, and I was on my way to another location. On my way back, I managed to catch a glimpse of a small sign sitting rather low to the ground and decided to make the turn.

The short length of dirt road turned quickly and brought me to a clearing. There I discovered a beautiful lake worthy of a paddle. Decorated with some short, red-rock cliffs on one side and grassy marsh on the other, Sheep Creek provides several dimensions to paddle.

While Sheep Creek is not large, it is not small either. There is certainly enough water to make the trip worthwhile, and the surrounding scenery really enhances the whole experience. Pines line the shore, and the Uintas delicately climb skyward in the background. In all, it is a scene that any paddler might enjoy.

In some ways, the undocumented location could provide a nice spot away from some of the other more popular locations that are nearby. Browne and Spirit lakes are both relatively close.

The water at Sheep Creek is somewhat protected, and thus, wind should not be a huge factor. There are a lot of shallows near the marshy shore, and the lake's shifting size during the season can make for some mud. In all, this is a great place to paddle and has all the elements for a perfect day.

Sheep Creek is in the High Uinta Range, and this means you need to prepare for pleasant days and cool nights with frequent mountain showers. At over 8,000 feet, the weather can be unpredictable and surprisingly cool even in the middle of summer.

The area is located off a lengthy dirt road that should not be taken by vehicles without a little bit of clearance. The road has rocks and is quite dusty, but a four-wheel-drive vehicle is not required.

Mountain wildlife is plentiful, and you can expect to see deer, birds of prey, and possibly some moose or elk. Bears and mountain lions exist; when camping, it is smart to take the proper precautions. Sheep Creek is a touch more isolated and less visited than some of the other surrounding waters and may be attractive to the larger animals.

It is also important to note that the name Sheep Creek is used often in the area. There is a Sheep Creek on Flaming Gorge, which is nearby. There is a Sheep Creek Loop, which is a scenic route to the lake, but is named for a canyon. Be certain to check the lake's location on a map before making a visit.

SMITH AND MOREHOUSE RESERVOIR

County: Summit
LONG/LAT: N40 45.310 W110 06.091
Elevation: 7,960 feet/2,426 meters
Body Type: Reservoir
Difficulty: Easy
Season: Spring, summer, autumn
Size: 44 acres
Directions: From Oakley, follow the Weber Canyon Drive until it reaches cabin property. Follow it to the right. Take the paved road up to the reservoir. The route from Oakley to the reservoir is well marked.
Put-in: There is a boat ramp on the south side of the reservoir, or access is relatively easy from the top of the dam.
Other Sports: Fishing, camping, bird-watching, hiking
Information: None

Paddle Overview

When you are sitting at your desk imagining yourself on a beautiful mountain lake—with quaking aspens, swaying pines, and the wind whistling through the trees—the place your brain has taken you is Smith and Morehouse. This picturesque reservoir, nestled up a canyon, gives every paddler a place to make dreams come true.

Smith and Morehouse is a high-elevation lake that is abundant in scenic beauty. Mountains tower over the reservoir on three of its four sides, protecting it from strong winds and the elements. You can expect a smooth surface and an easy paddle through most of the season.

Located just above Oakley, this reservoir is a popular spot and gets some campers and paddlers throughout the summer. There is some excellent camping below and above the reservoir. However, because of the steep mountain slopes, there are no waterfront camping spots. I have also found some terrific picnic spots and great hikes along the shore.

At one spot, my daughter and I hopped out of our boat and found a little glen with a small beaver dam. A few felled trees and some driftwood

Boats and driftwood at Smith and Moorehouse

created a small pond. We explored the area and found many lovely wildflowers and some great shade from the sun.

You may not be able to camp on the water, but getting your boat on the water is a breeze. A boat launch is located on a road that runs along the west side. You can also put in on the dam, which is rocky, but relatively easy to trek across. Either way, Smith and Morehouse is easy to access.

While Smith and Morehouse is not enormous, it certainly is adequate for paddling. You will find ample space to test your muscles. The only fault I can recall is the shape, which is typically oblong and limited in features. You can see the far end of the reservoir from the dam, and thus, you know what to expect.

The great thing about Smith and Morehouse is that it is relatively close to the Wasatch Front. You can be in this perfect setting in less than two hours from Salt Lake City. In fact, many people make this a summer-home location. As you drive to the reservoir, you will see numerous cabins and entrances to cabin property.

You will understand the attraction for all these homes. This is really a perfect spot. You can't ask for a prettier paddle; it is easy to access, and you can find some great places to explore. You see, dreams really can come true.

FLAMING GORGE RESERVOIR

County: Daggett
LONG/LAT: N40 54.878 W109 25.663
Elevation: 6,023 feet/1,836 meters
Body Type: Reservoir
Difficulty: Difficult
Season: Spring, summer, autumn
Size: 42,000 acres
Directions: From Vernal, drive north on US 191. At the corner of US 191 and UT 44, take either the right or the left route. UT 44 will take you to Manila. US 191 will take you to Dutch John. Marinas are in both areas.
Put-in: There is a marina just outside Manila in Sheep Creek Bay. There are a number of campgrounds along the shore of the reservoir. You can also find a boat ramp in Lucerne. On the opposite end, there is a marina near Mustang Ridge.
Other Sports: Fishing, camping, hiking, climbing, swimming
Information: 435-789-1181

Paddle Overview

Flaming Gorge is a massive body of water formed by a dam on the Green River. This recreation area has its bottom in Utah, and its fingers extend northward into Wyoming. While a lot of the water in these red canyons is in Wyoming, the predominant recreational access and best scenery is in Utah.

Close to the dam, you can find a small island and many small canyons to explore. Discovery is one of the great pleasures of paddling Flaming Gorge. You can find innumerable spots to take your boat and explore. In fact, a multi-day trip is ideal because shore camping is allowed and you will have time to really explore all this area has to offer.

There are many notable canyons to visit on a paddle. Sheep Creek and Horseshoe canyons are known for their beauty and stunning cliff heights. Horseshoe is quite narrow and loops around, allowing you to return to your starting spot and make a base camp. Kingfisher Island is another fascinating spot that you can drop into before heading over to Hideout Canyon.

Paddling this area provides unparalleled exhilaration while you glance upward at cliffs that rival the tallest manufactured structures in the world. Add to this the innumerable canyons and coves to explore, and you have found one of the best places to paddle in the state.

Of all the areas to visit, the Red Canyon, named by explorer John Wesley Powell, is certainly the greatest spectacle. Climbing nearly 1,000 feet, the cliffs are densely forested, and the green contrasts with the underlying red rock. The steep incline is fascinating from above at the visitor center or from below on the water. With a single glance you understand how the place got the name Flaming Gorge.

One detraction to the area is its popularity. Flaming Gorge rivals Lake Powell as a summer destination, and it can get very busy from June through August. You can expect abundant powerboat activity during the summer, which means that there will be a lot of chop in areas near the marina and potential safety risks from fast-moving watercraft.

This location is not for novices. Even the best paddlers will need to be prepared for the massive size of Flaming Gorge. You may have to paddle several miles to find the right camping spot; day trips, while possible are not as enjoyable. Before venturing on this body of water, I suggest investing in detailed maps and planning your trip carefully.

In addition, Flaming Gorge has a wind problem. Because of the scale and narrowness of the canyons, the wind can build serious chop on the water. Two- to three-foot swells are not unheard of; unless you are experienced in that kind of water, it can be very dangerous.

While visiting the gorge, you may want to catch one of the many thrilling river trips that are run out of Dutch John. These take you below the dam and provide a white-water rafting experience. The price for these trips includes transportation to and from the river. Many venture more than 7 miles downriver and hit rapids of various sizes.

If you are looking for a paddle trip that will provide an experience of a lifetime, consider the gorge. Its massive red cliffs, excellent camping, and warm water are inviting, exciting, and ready for exploration.

ECHO RESERVOIR

County: Summit
LONG/LAT: N40 55.390 W111 24.243
Elevation: 5,560 feet/1,695 meters
Body Type: Reservoir
Difficulty: Moderate
Season: Spring, summer, autumn
Size: 1,394 acres
Directions: From Park City, take I-80 to exit 164 at Coalville. Head east and drive into downtown Coalville. Continue north to the reservoir.
Put-in: The road that hugs the eastern shoreline has numerous spots to drop in a boat. I prefer to stay on the south side and look for a beach or parking spot that keeps me in this area.
Other Sports: Fishing, camping, bird-watching, swimming
Information: www.recreation.gov/detail.cfm?ID=1186

The Uinta Range is home to moose, elk, and deer.

Paddle Overview

Echo is an interesting place. It is a popular spot for powerboaters, but excellent for paddlers as well. It is rare when both types of boaters can share a lake, because the wake and speed of powerboating usually make paddling difficult. However, Echo provides an easily accessible and interesting paddle.

On the south end, the Weber River feeds the reservoir. Before the water gets deep enough, there is a large amount of marshy wetlands with nice flat paddling as the river twists, turns, and undulates into the reservoir. This area is rarely touched by traffic, and it is exciting to explore.

Another appealing aspect of paddling in there is the constantly shifting and changing landscape. As the water rises and lowers, the shape and paddling dimensions change. Land masses form, and areas that were once underwater become islands. In addition, the flow of the river changes, and new areas become covered with water.

You can always find a lot of attractive aspects to paddling at Echo; while the Weber can have a strong current, it is fun to paddle upstream, if even for a short while. The flow of the river, combined with the interesting landscape, sometimes throws in a challenge, but nothing that a decent paddler can't handle.

Echo has a crescent shape, and the canyon winds make the northwest section near the dam by far the most challenging area to paddle. Add the boat traffic and the high shoreline, and this is one spot you may want to avoid entirely. Of course, those with a sense of adventure may want to tackle this challenge.

Echo is conveniently located close to Salt Lake and Ogden. If you are looking to make a quick trip, and you stick to the shallows, Echo is easy to access and has some great opportunities to explore.

OTHER DESTINATIONS

BEAVER LAKE
County: Summit
LONG/LAT: N40 49.609 W110 56.476
Size: 3 acres
Directions: From Kamas, Beaver Lake is located off UT 150. You will need to trek 7 miles via rough dirt road. The dirt road is located just past Hayden Fork Campground, on your left. Signs to Beaver exist just below Whitney Reservoir.
Comment: A pretty little lake near Whitney Reservoir, this place is very isolated and very small. If you make the trek to Whitney, there is no reason not to visit Beaver, but there is not much to paddle.

BUTTERFLY LAKE

County: Duchesne

LONG/LAT: N40 43.245 W110 52.092

Size: 5 acres

Directions: From Kamas, Butterfly Lake is located on UT 150 at Hayden Pass, 3 miles north of Mirror Lake.

Comment: Butterfly earns its name from its distinctive shape. Two wing-shaped bodies of water are slightly bisected by a jutting peninsula. This small but fun orientation makes for a delightful paddle off the Mirror Lake Highway.

LILY LAKE AND TEAPOT LAKE

County: Summit

LONG/LAT: N40 40.826 W110 56.322

Size: 3 acres

Directions: From Kamas, Lily and Teapot are located on the west side of UT 150, just off the road across from Lost Lake.

Comment: Lily and Teapot are adjacent to one another on the west side of the Mirror Lake Highway. Both are very small, and while neither offers much in the way of a paddle, they are so cute you may be tempted. It will only take you a second to get across, but the scenery just might be worth it.

LILY LAKE #2

County: Summit

LONG/LAT: N40 52.740 W110 48.637

Size: 4 acres

Directions: From Kamas, Lily Lake #2 is located off UT 150, just past the ranger station on your right. Take the right heading west for a bit and then backtrack south for 2 to 3 miles of really rough dirt road, which will bring you to the lake. The road to Lily #2 is also a RV dump stop and is clearly marked.

Comment: The setting is lovely, and lily pads are in abundance. However, the drive is a bit scary. With an inappropriate vehicle, the large rocks and multiple ruts make the 2-mile journey feel like it will last forever.

LOST LAKE

County: Summit
LONG/LAT: N40 40.818 W110 56.258
Size: 35 acres
Directions: From Kamas, Lost Lake is located on UT 150 on the east side, just off the road across from Lily and Teapot.
Comment: Lost is not nearly as scenic as the other lakes on the Mirror Lake Highway, but it is a decent-sized lake with a very convenient parking lot. In addition, the put-in is a breeze. Yet compared to all the choices available, Lost is not an attractive destination.

LYMAN LAKE

County: Summit
LONG/LAT: N40 56.465 W110 36.493
Size: 27 acres
Directions: From Kamas, Lyman Lake is located off UT 150, about 1 mile past the ranger station on your right. The road is near the gate for winter closings, and you will see signs for a Boy Scout camp. The 20-mile washboard road will bring you to the lake. The road is well traveled and goes over Elizabeth Pass at 10,235 feet. Lyman is clearly marked with signs.
Comment: I struggled with not including Lyman as a Best Bet. It is a terrific spot and, generally speaking, one of the best small lakes in the region. However, 45 minutes of washboard dirt road is a serious detraction. If you have a vehicle that can handle the long rough road, definitely make this a stop.

PASS LAKE

County: Duchesne

LONG/LAT: N40 42.761 W110 53.633

Size: 10 acres

Directions: From Kamas, Pass Lake is located on UT 150 about 1 mile north of Mirror Lake.

Comment: The real issue with Pass Lake is not its scenery or size. Both are nice, and the lake is quite an attractive paddle. However, there doesn't seem to be a decent portage to get your boat to the water. From the parking lot you will have to navigate a series of narrow paths to get to the water's edge. If you are willing to do a little work, it might be a rewarding paddle.

ROCKPORT RESERVOIR

County: Summit

LONG/LAT: N40 45.233 W111 22.446

Size: 1,189 acres

Directions: From Park City, follow I-80 west to the Wanship exit (#156). Follow UT 32 south for about 1.5 miles. The reservoir is easy to spot on the east side of the road.

Comment: Rockport is a large reservoir close to Coalville and Kamas. Popular with the powerboaters, Rockport has limited paddle opportunities. There are some rookeries and marshland on the south end that are interesting to explore.

TRIAL LAKE

County: Summit

LONG/LAT: N40 40.759 W110 57.359

Size: 98 acres

Directions: From Kamas, Trial Lake is located on UT 150, on the west side, just off the road. Make a right and an immediate left into the parking lot by the dam.

Comment: Trial is a sister lake to Washington. They are right next to each other, and you can easily access either one from the same road. Trial is surprisingly large, and because of its proximity to the road, it gets a lot more traffic. It is a nice spot, but you might find Washington less crowded and more scenic.

WHITNEY RESERVOIR

County: Summit
LONG/LAT: N40 50.633 W110 55.826
Size: 3 acres
Directions: From Kamas, Whitney is located off UT 150. You will need to trek 7 miles via rough dirt road. The dirt road is located just past Hayden Fork Campground, on your left.
Comment: Whitney is a large, exposed reservoir with limited tree coverage, but easy access. It is a beautiful high-elevation spot with ample surface area. Yet it lacks features and is relatively plain for its location. If you don't mind the long dusty drive, it is a decent spot to paddle.

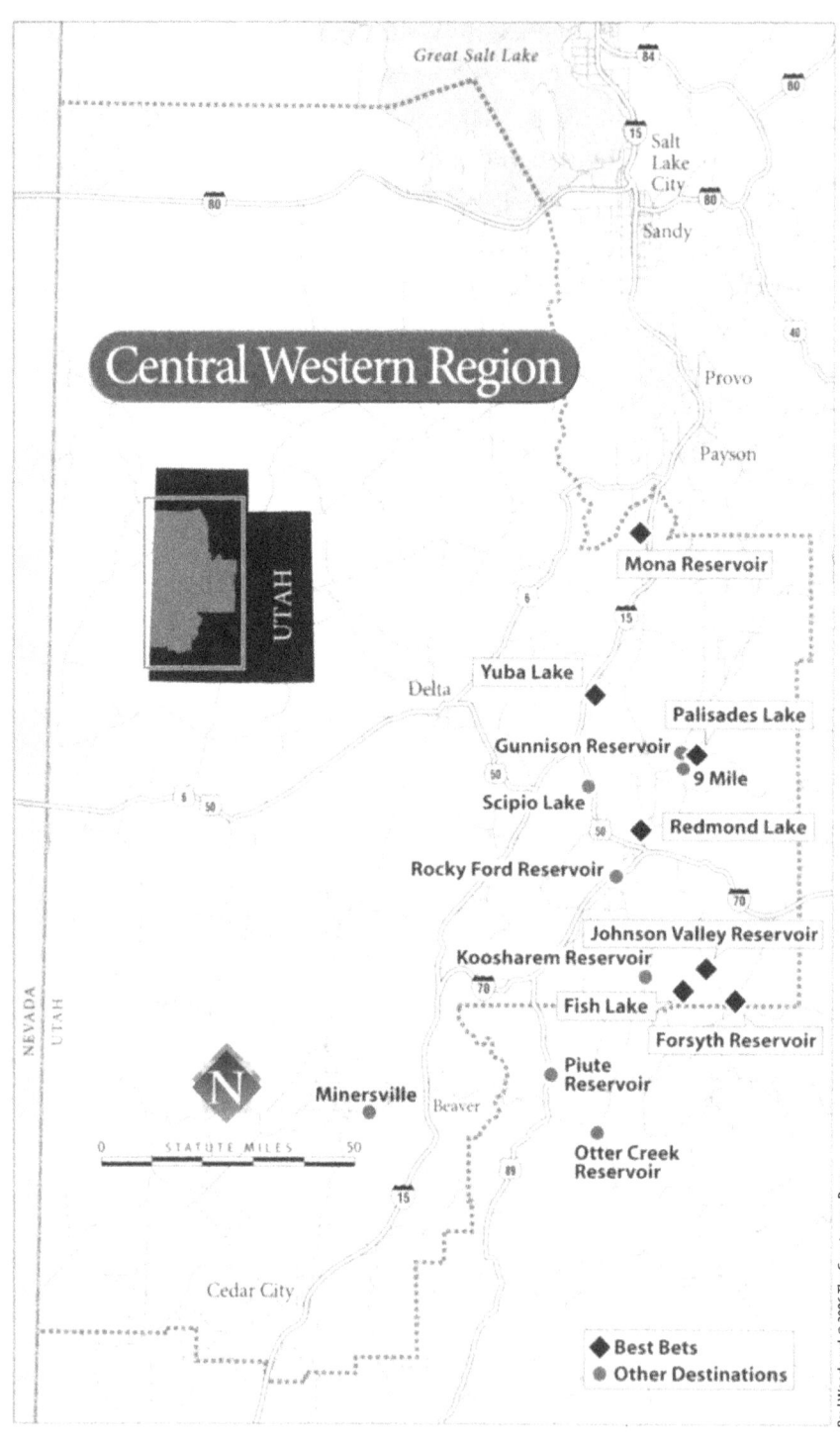

There are many tiny lakes east of Beaver in the Fishlake National Forest.

Central Western Region

The Central Western Region covers a lot of different terrain and types of paddling. The central section actually has a majority of the interesting paddles; while not all of it is wonderful, there are some delightful spots. In contrast, the western section has virtually no paddle spots that are worth driving the miles of road to access.

The fascinating thing about this place is the fact that while it covers the greatest amount of terrain of the regions I have noted in the book, it has the smallest number of good choices to paddle. Most of the land is desert, and most of the available paddling is focused on being an irrigation tool before being a recreational spot.

This is not to say that there aren't some good paddles in this region. In fact, there are some terrific spots. The best of the paddle destinations are closer to the mountains or located near the I-15 corridor. However, you may want to think carefully before making a trek westward.

The portion of the state known as the west desert is a barren and isolated place that holds little interest for paddlers. There are a few locations that have water, but these places are intended less for recreation and more for irrigation. The western desert of Utah is not really meant to be paddled. The U.S. government uses the northern portion of the desert as a practice bombing range.

The towns in the western region are small and isolated and have few services for a visitor. Many of the roads are neglected or entirely unpaved. The nature of this region is illustrated by the fact that there are only four paved roads that cross the western border into Nevada.

In my exploration of the region, I incurred damage to my car trying to get to a few of the remote spots and, in some cases, had to turn back. The simple fact is the landscape and water are not significant enough to note. I will spend most of this section trying to emphasize the locations that I believe will take you to the best paddling.

The central portion of the region has a lot of places to paddle. However, they are spread out and limited. Most are exposed mountain locations with sagebrush and hardly any trees. The wind blows often, and while the water works for paddling, the work of paddling isn't worthwhile.

If you venture forth in the Central Western Region, do not be discouraged by the features of the landscape. There are some lovely spots that are first rate. The entire region is not a loss for paddling. These destinations exist between the north and the south. Thus, you can discover places to put your boat in as you trek across the state.

Of the cities in this region, Cedar City is by far the largest and certainly could be considered one of the prettiest. Cedar City is a gateway to many terrific paddle spots and national parks. This charming little hamlet along the mountains is known as the Festival City. Because of its renowned Utah Shakespearean Festival, many tourists frequent it throughout the summer.

The Shakespearean festival is known across the country, and possibly the world, as one of the finest this nation has to offer. Every summer, the festival stages four to six different plays. The festival has a small reproduction of the Globe Theater, which hosts the outdoor productions. Top professional actors and a beautiful theater complex make this festival a must-visit event if you are in the area.

Cedar City is well suited to visitors and travelers. The newly renovated downtown is popular spot for people to dine and shop. There are ample hotels; because the city is also home to Southern Utah State University, it is well accommodated.

Northwest in the Sevier River Valley, a unique resort called the Big Rock Candy Mountain resides just off I-70 on US 89. This sulphur-and-stone mountain has the appearance of a large candy structure. The resort rests along the river and offers a lot of fun recreational activities. One of its newest features is a paved 7.5-mile bike trail that follows the old train tracks.

To the north, Nephi is most known as the last stop along the Wasatch Mountains on your way to the central part of the state. For visitors heading south, it is a common spot to fill up on food and gas. Once you pass Nephi, services are sparse for many miles. There are a number of decent restaurants just off the interstate.

Trekking west, Delta is the largest rural town in western Utah. If you have just had enough water, northeast of Delta is the Little Sahara Recreation Area. This is a popular spot with ATV riders, who want to cruise the large sand dunes. Covering 120 square miles, the area is fascinating to explore.

Beaver is one of the larger cities in the central part of the state. It is an excellent starting point if you want to be centrally located in this region. There are numerous tiny mountain lakes to the east in the

Fishlake National Forest, and just south you can drop over to US 89 from UT 20, giving you access to many of the reservoirs on Sevier Plateau.

While the Central Western Region is not exactly a paddler's heaven, there are some little spots of heaven. Its deserts are large, but its mountains are beautiful. The region has a long history of mining, and as with that activity, you may have to do a little digging to find that special spot.

BEST BETS

MONA RESERVOIR

County: Juab

LONG/LAT: N39 52.521 W111 52.332

Elevation: 4,490 feet/1,369 meters

Body Type: Reservoir

Difficulty: Easy

Season: Spring, summer, autumn

Size: 1,100 acres

Directions: From I-15, take the Mona-Goshen exit and follow the road east. You will pass through town and then follow the road to the north. Follow Goshen Canyon Road to the west side of the reservoir. There is a dirt road with a cattle guard about 5 miles on your right. Follow this road, and it will take you down to the reservoir.

Put-in: There is a boat ramp on the western side of the reservoir. There is no access from the east.

Other Sports: Fishing, camping, swimming, hiking, bird-watching

Information: www.go-utah.com/mona-reservoir

Paddle Overview

Located just off the interstate, Mona is an appealing location because it is as good as it looks. Set up against a small mountain, the reservoir is very attractive in its surroundings. As you fly by at 80 miles per hour, you might think that it would be a good spot for a paddle. Perhaps it is time to stop and give it a try.

Mona, a small mountain reservoir, sits under the shadow of Mount Nebo.

This long reservoir sits under the shadow of Mount Nebo, the largest mountain on the Wasatch Range. At nearly 12,000 feet (3,657 meters), the mountain towers over this countrified valley. It is a stunning mountain that provides terrific decoration for Mona Reservoir.

Even without Mount Nebo, Mona is a lovely spot for paddling. Its gentle waters and lengthy form recline against the mountains and invite you to paddle. The soft, marshy shore provides a spot that is quiet yet interesting to explore by boat. Mona provides every feature you might want for a nice day on the water.

Accessing the water is a touch confusing if you do not follow the directions. There are some nice facilities at the lake, but by looking at the map, you might consider trying to approach from the east or north. The west side is the only access, and it is not well marked.

There is a boat ramp and primitive camping close to the water, and up above you will find some nice picnic spots with excellent views of the reservoir and valley. I started the day in the early morning and found the place empty. The entire reservoir was left alone for a solitary paddle.

Another discovery we made while on our visit to this area was the large population of hawks. We saw no less than a dozen of these majestic and beautiful birds keeping watch for their morning meal. They seem to congregate along the road to the reservoir, and we spent a long time just watching them patrol the farmlands to the west.

On the opposite side of the reservoir, you will find the Young Living Farm. This organic farm provides a number of activities for the whole family—pony rides and herb gardens in a peaceful setting. They specialize in essential oils and provide tours that educate you in the distillation process.

If you decide to stop, note that the area gets windy, but the water is fairly shallow and should not generate a huge chop. In fact, these shallow levels keep the water quite warm during the summer months. Mona is certainly a great spot to paddle and worth the short drive from the interstate.

REDMOND LAKE

County: Sevier
LONG/LAT: N38 59.900 W111 52.249
Elevation: 5,110 feet/1,558 meters
Body Type: Lake
Difficulty: Easy
Season: Spring, summer, autumn
Size: 160 acres
Directions: From Salina, head north on UT 256. In Redmond, the road turns into State Street. Take a left on 300 South. Head west until it curves around to the south. The lake is on the left.

Put-in: On the northeast corner there is a parking area that leads directly to the shore. Look for a tall isolated tree to the south.

Other Sports: Fishing, camping, bird-watching, hiking, climbing, swimming

Information: None

Paddle Overview

One of the best parts of authoring this book was the surprises. When I saw Redmond on a map, I was not inclined to make the trek to it. The small little blue spot on the diagram indicated marsh and swamp with little water. To make matters worse, irrigation ponds and a river that seemed to be going the wrong direction misled me. Yet once I finally did find the lake, I was astonished.

The map I used does not adequately portray Redmond Lake, which has large amounts of marsh and swamp combined with a beautiful expanse of open water. It is a subtle, idyllic spot with a lot more than what you initially see. Large trees adorn some portions of the shore, while tall grasses decorate the farthest regions of the lake. Marshy islands and narrow passages further expand the interesting and exciting elements to paddle.

In the distance, the Black Mountains and their foothills decorate the skyline. The rural setting combined with the stunning backdrop provides a great setting for a paddle. There is a little coverage over to the north, and the water appears to be fairly protected from the winds by the Valley Mountains. The south end is wide open and stretches out across the valley.

Redmond is purely a paddle location. There are no facilities, and the depth of the water prevents powerboats from using it. Thus, you can expect your visit will be quiet, serene, and uninterrupted. The relative isolation of the location should also provide at least some moments of exclusivity. I did not see another soul, and I imagine this is common.

My visit was in late summer, and the water level was quite good. Spring should make the paddle surface even larger and more appealing.

Some large trees adorn the shore at Redmond Lake.

Bird-watching should also be spectacular in the spring and autumn. This is one of many wetlands sporadically located between various smaller mountain ranges in central Utah.

The town of Redmond is only a short drive from the city of Salina. Redmond is predominantly homes, but Salina is a charming yet modest town with a truly American feel. Mom's Café and the five-and-dime still exist, and farmers sitting on sidewalk benches chat about the crops.

Salina is a popular stop off I-70 because it is the first location in a shortcut north through Scipio to the Wasatch Front. Taking US 50 will shave significant miles if you are heading north from I-70 to I-15. And while Redmond is off this route, it is a worthwhile diversion that you should definitely consider. Trust me when I tell you that you will be pleasantly surprised.

YUBA LAKE (SEVIER BRIDGE RESERVOIR)

County: Juab, Sanpete
LONG/LAT: N39 24.247 W112 01.464
Elevation: 4,954 feet/1,510 meters
Body Type: Reservoir
Difficulty: Difficult
Season: Spring, summer, autumn, winter
Size: 10,905 acres
Directions: NORTH: From Nephi, take I-15 south for 20 miles to the Yuba Lake exit (#202) and drive about 2 miles south to the lake. EAST: From Nephi, take UT 28. Follow the road south through Levan for 13 miles. Follow the signs for the state-park entrance.
Put-in: There is a boat launch at the east entrance. Both locations have nice sandy beaches for shore paddling.
Other Sports: Fishing, camping, swimming, bird-watching
Information: www.stateparks.utah.gov/park_pages/parkpage.php?id=ysp

Paddle Overview

The dunes and beaches of Yuba Lake were the first thing that captivated me about the place. The large windswept formations are unique when compared to any other body of water I have paddled in Utah. The soft and subtle beauty, combined with the tremendous size of the lake, makes it a fascinating destination to explore.

The challenge of Yuba is the combination of wind and size. The fourth-largest manufactured body of water in the state, it covers nearly 11,000 acres. The lake starts on the south near Fayette and heads north. The area has a large wetland before it opens into the reservoir.

Yuba is definitely a windy spot. The wind creates some chop on the water and causes sand to get everywhere. Even a short visit will have you shaking out the boat when you get home. However, this is a minor inconvenience when considering the beautiful and unique landscape.

Patterns in the beach at Yuba Lake

If you are worried about the size, there is another entrance to the park on the southeast side of the reservoir where the wind is lighter and the water is much more manageable. The beach is nice, but the dunes are not as interesting. This area is closer to the Sevier River.

The lake has some interesting peninsulas and a few islands. However, it is going to take some serious strength to explore everything this lake has to offer. Camping is available at both parks; if you want to truly experience the place, you may want to consider spending a couple of days.

The water had obviously been collecting in the area long before the settlers first constructed a dam in 1907. Many people have discovered Native American artifacts in the region. In addition, there are remnants of mining operations and early ranching along the lake's shores.

The advanced paddler may find a real challenge by floating from the northwest corner to the southeast and back again, though I have never done this. The 6-mile round-trip journey from one park to the other could provide a fun weekend on the water. Load your boat and gear on one end, camp one night, and then paddle back.

Almost everything about Yuba is soft. The warm water, sandy beaches, excellent facilities, and gentle scenery are alluring. Yet at the same time, the place can provide a real challenge for the experienced paddler because of its large size and windy surface. In all, it is a great place for all and sundry.

JOHNSON VALLEY RESERVOIR
County: Sevier
LONG/LAT: N38 37.133 W111 38.532
Elevation: 8,734 feet/2,662 meters
Body Type: Reservoir
Difficulty: Moderate
Season: Summer
Size: 704 acres
Directions: From Loa, head north on UT 72. About 8 miles out of town, take a left on to UT 25. You will pass Mill Meadow and continue up the mountain for about 25 miles. The entrance to the reservoir will be on your left just after you come over the ridge.
Put-in: The boat ramp on the east side is ideal because it provides parking and easy access to a reservoir that has a lot of rocky shore.
Other Sports: Fishing, camping, bird-watching
Information: None

Paddle Overview

Located at the top of the Fish Lake Plateau, just north and a little east of Fish Lake, this scenic lake is like a baby brother to Fish Lake. Many of the same features that make Fish Lake a popular spot are also available at Johnson Valley. However, Johnson Valley is about a tenth of Fish Lake's size and less crowded.

The scenic little brother of Fish Lake, Johnson Valley is much less crowded.

Johnson Valley is set in a stunning valley. Abundant trees and striking mountain ridges surround the water. The reservoir has a very simple layout and limited paddle features to explore. Yet this really doesn't matter as your eye is drawn to the surrounding landscape.

The facilities at the lake are relatively simple. However, they are perfect for a short day trip. There is a boat ramp and nice picnic area on the eastern shore. If you are planning a longer stay, campsites are located across the road to the north.

One fascinating aspect to explore is the abundant volcanic rock located on the eastern shore. These massive and unique black rocks decorate a large portion of the shoreline. They are just one of the many interesting geological forms in the region.

If you come from the Fish Lake side, you need to keep driving. Just over the ridge is the Gooseberry-Fremont Scenic Backway. This is a terrific drive that should not be missed. The winding road navigates down a mountain path and through a stunning river valley. This is also the route to other paddle spots and to the city of Loa.

The area is predominantly used during the summer. The high elevations make it difficult to access other times of the year. Because of the short season, you may want to consider Johnson Valley as a side trip while on a visit to the region. It is a great place to paddle; while it may not be as large as Fish Lake, this scenic reservoir has just as much charm.

FISH LAKE

County: Sevier
LONG/LAT: N38 32.068 W111 44.179
Elevation: 8,730 feet/2,661 meters
Body Type: Lake
Difficulty: Moderate to difficult
Season: Summer
Size: 11,520 acres

Directions: From Salina, take US 89 south to UT 24, then follow UT 24 south through Sigurd to UT 25. Take a left onto UT 25 and head northeast until you reach the lake.

Put-in: There are multiple spots suitable to put in. Two marinas and a large shoreline are easy to access.

Other Sports: Fishing, camping, hiking

Information: www.fishlake.com; www.utah.com/nationalsites/fishlake.htm

Paddle Overview

Most natural mountain lakes in Utah are high elevation and quite small. They are also very difficult to access and often require a hike or miles of off-road travel. This is why Fish Lake is so special. A giant natural mountain lake, it is easy to access and a joy to paddle.

Fish Lake sits in a national forest named after it. The lake has a beauty especially rare in this region of the state. Surrounded by throngs of quaking aspens and evergreen trees, the lake rings true in the heart of every paddler. The moment you turn the corner and grab a view of the lake, your fingers itch to grab your paddle.

One of the nicest traits of the lake is that its natural layout creates excellent areas for paddlers to explore while keeping out of the way of all the summer visitors in fishing boats. On the northern half, the water becomes marshy, and a small bay is created.

Widgeon Bay has a wonderful surface area and is distant from the more popular areas to the south. Because the area is somewhat weedy and there is a bit of mud, you may want to put in at the Bowery Haven Marina and paddle into the bay. The narrow channel that separates the lake and bay is only a short paddle from the marina.

Of course, the entire lake is very suitable for paddling. At 6 miles long and 1 mile wide, it has more than enough space for everyone. The surface is large, and choppy conditions are certainly possible. However, the lake is known for its glassy smooth surface.

Novice paddlers might be intimidated by the lake's large size and limited features. However, experienced paddlers will want to get an early

Plan ahead if booking the popular rustic cabins at Fish Lake.

start before the more casual boaters get on the lake. Because the water is deep and quite cold, people typically do not swim or waterski.

However, the high-elevation temperatures do not discourage visitors. In fact, there are a number of lodges and campgrounds available at Fish Lake. Because of its popularity as a summer vacation destination, you may want to consider booking early if you opt to rent a rustic cabin. The lake is accessible for paddling only between June and October, and the area fills quickly. Even finding a campground can be a challenge, so plan ahead.

Beyond the traditional fishing that lures most people to the lake, area activities include hiking and biking. In fact, a bike trail surrounds the lake and provides an easy opportunity to see its natural beauty on the north side. The south side is for the serious mountain biker.

Fish Lake is a diverse and beautiful destination that provides everything you could want in a paddle vacation. From its large size to the smooth surface, this lake provides all the elements for a good paddle.

FORSYTH RESERVOIR

County: Sevier
LONG/LAT: N38 31.218 W111 31.706
Elevation: 7,969 feet/2,429 meters
Body Type: Reservoir
Difficulty: Difficult
Season: Spring, summer, autumn
Size: 158 acres
Directions: From Loa, head north on UT 72. The road goes a short distance past the reservoir. Make a left onto the short dirt road, and follow it to the reservoir.
Put-in: There is an unimproved boat ramp on the peninsula in the middle of the reservoir. Directly next to the ramp is parking.
Other Sports: Fishing, camping, swimming, hiking, bird-watching
Information: None

Paddle Overview

As I noted in the introduction to the Central Western Region, many of the lakes in this region are very similar. In fact, throughout the area the landscape seems identical. Sagebrush hills surrounding a reservoir with infrequent trees represent the typical appearance of these places. Forsyth follows suit, but it has something unique to offer paddlers.

Located in the middle of the reservoir is a long flat peninsula; while this alone makes the paddling more interesting, it is not the only factor that makes the reservoir attractive. There are high embankments and a few more trees, and as such, I feel it is a worthy paddle.

On my visit we saw numerous people out on the water taking a spin in their kayaks. Obviously, the appeal of this place is not exclusive to me. I noted the reservoir's well-protected form on my visit and saw a lot interesting places to take a boat. By no means is Forsyth the most incredible paddle in this region, but it is certainly worth trying.

In addition, the Desert View Overlook is located a short distance up UT 72. From there you can view the north end of Capitol Reef National Park. This spectacular sight has amazing red plateaus jutting upward from the landscape. The scenery is reminiscent of the old Western films.

This north-end view of Capitol Reef is just a short drive from Forsyth.

Forsyth is basically a desert paddle. The place offers no services, and you have to take out anything you bring in. However, if you are interested in experiencing one of these sagebrush-laden desert paddles, this is the one to pick.

PALISADES LAKE

County: Sanpete
LONG/LAT: N39 15.321 W111 39.421
Elevation: 5,868 feet/1,789 meters
Body Type: Reservoir
Difficulty: Easy
Season: Spring, summer, autumn, winter
Size: 66 acres
Directions: From Manti, head south on US 89. The entrance to the park is a few miles out of town, on the east side. Turn left into the entrance.
Put-in: You can simply drop in your boat from the shore or use the pier.
Other Sports: Fishing, camping, swimming
Information: www.stateparks.utah.gov/park_pages/parkpage.php?id=pssp

Paddle Overview

Palisades is a historic location. It has been in existence since 1899, when the Mormon pioneers settled the region. Building the dam with manual labor, they created this small reservoir to help irrigate their new settlement in the Sanpete Valley. What remains today is a nice state park with a small golf course and ample camping.

The reservoir is not immense, and there are no real features that I could note. However, it is focused on paddling. In fact, canoe rentals are available, and on my visit, there were numerous people out enjoying the water. It is too small for anything else.

Beach, pier, and excellent facilities—all the conveniences of a state park at Palisades

The reservoir features a nice sandy beach and a pier. There are numerous shady spots and excellent camping. The nice thing about Palisades is that it provides a spot to paddle with all the conveniences of the state park.

Just south of Manti, this reservoir is situated in a historical area. This region is steeped in Mormon history. Manti was the first white settlement in the region. Because many of the original structures from the settlement remain, you can get an excellent sense of what life was like here more than 150 years ago.

Manti has one of the original Mormon temples in Utah, and this structure is impossible to miss. Sitting atop a tall hill, this beautiful building is fascinating, considering it was completed in 1888. The structure remains very well preserved and pre-dates the dedication of the Salt Lake City Temple. Mormons do not allow nonmembers to enter, but the architecture is fascinating, especially in such a rural setting.

Palisades is not too far from other paddling locations that you might want to try. Gunnison, 9 Mile, and Wales are a short drive from the park. These bodies of water have few features and are not ideal, but their close proximity may encourage you to explore their waters.

In all, Palisades is a great spot for a paddling trip bundled with a family vacation. While the region is not an ideal spot to paddle, Palisades does everything right to make paddling an enjoyable experience.

OTHER DESTINATIONS

9 MILE
County: Sanpete
LONG/LAT: N39 10.323 W111 42.348
Size: 213 acres
Directions: From Manti, head south on US 89 about 6 miles to just before the UT 137 junction.
Comment: Located directly off US 89, 9 Mile is nothing more than a small pond with some bland scenery and few features to explore. In fact, if it weren't so convenient, it wouldn't be worth paddling. Palisades State Park is a short trek north and a much prettier spot.

DMAD RESERVOIR (DELTA RESERVOIR)
County: Millard
LONG/LAT: N39 39.8333 W112 47.2778
Size: 1,199 acres

Animals live even in desert conditions. The river landscape is an excellent place to spot wildlife.

Directions: From Delta, head north on US 6. Just past the airport, there is access via a dirt road on the right.

Comment: DMAD was one reservoir that I really wanted to explore, but just could not get the time. Because of its extreme western location, it is off the main routes to most of the places I visited. While it is located in the west desert, it appears to have interesting features, including some islands. If you are out that way, you may want to explore this large reservoir.

Sheep are still a common sight on Utah's landscape.

GUNNISON RESERVOIR

County: Sanpete

LONG/LAT: N39 12.370 W111 42.472

Size: 1,287 acres

Directions: From Manti, head south on US 89 for about 3 miles. Turn right on Gunnison Reservoir Road and head west. The road is dirt and winds around about 1 mile before it gets to the reservoir.

Comment: I was quite excited to see and visit Gunnison. It looks fairly large on the map and is in a waterfowl-management area. After my visit, I think it is best left untracked. Apparently the place dries up often and is basically a mud hole. Water levels were quite low, and other than some decent-looking mountain cliffs, the place is fairly nondescript.

KOOSHAREM RESERVOIR

County: Sevier
LONG/LAT: N38 35.984 W111 50.797
Size: 310 acres
Directions: From Loa, head northwest on UT 24 and go just past UT 62. The reservoir is directly off to your right about 20 miles.
Comment: Yet another highly exposed reservoir along a mountainside, Koosharem is more interesting in name than in paddling. Keep driving up the mountain to Fish Lake and the surrounding area if you want a much prettier spot and more interesting details.

MILL MEADOW

County: Sevier, Wayne
LONG/LAT: N38 30.931 W111 33.846
Size: 156 acres
Directions: From Loa, head north on UT 72. Pass through Fremont and take a left on UT 25. The reservoir is on the west side of the road about 2 miles up.
Comment: It is not that Mill Meadow is bad, it is that there are so many better spots within a short drive. Forsyth is much more attractive for paddling, and you are only a short drive from the Fish Lake National Forest. I would suggest passing up Mill Meadow unless you have crowds at one of the other locations.

MINERSVILLE

County: Beaver
LONG/LAT: N38 13.103 W112 49.793
Size: 990 acres

Directions: From Beaver, head west on UT 21 about 12 miles. The entrance is on the southwest side of the reservoir. Access is possible from the north via a dirt road through Adamsville.

Comment: Minersville is a desert reservoir with a lot of space and little appeal for paddling. Most of its use is for powerboating; while its long form keeps people apart, it has nothing distinguishing to offer a paddler. The one benefit is that it is not used a lot, so it might be a good spot for a quiet paddle, especially during midweek.

OTTER CREEK RESERVOIR

County: Piute
LONG/LAT: N38 10.032 W112 01.052
Size: 2,520 acres

Directions: From Loa, head northwest on UT 24, take a left onto UT 62, and head south for about 30 miles. The reservoir is on the left and is well marked.

Comment: Otter Creek is massive, and on my visit, exceptionally windy. The place resides in a flat valley, and I expect that the wind is a frequent problem. It is a great size, and if you are looking for a challenging paddle, it might be a worthy destination. If you can, take the pass from Piute to Otter Creek via Kingston Canyon. It's a wonderful drive.

PIUTE RESERVOIR

County: Piute
LONG/LAT: N38 19.553 W112 13.125
Size: 2,508 acres

Directions: From I-70 at Sevier, head south on US 89, passing through Marysville. The reservoir is on the left just before Junction. Turn east at the state-park entrance.

Comment: Piute is a large reservoir in a nice setting. It is close to the Sevier River, and the scenery is a wide open valley with a very rural appeal. There is a state park at the location, and it gets used.

However, the water is very large, and there is no doubt that you can find some quiet paddling during midweek.

ROCKY FORD RESERVOIR
County: Sevier
LONG/LAT: N38 52.105 W111 57.400
Size: Approximately 125 acres (drained)
Directions: From Salina, head south on US 89. Follow the east route to UT 24. There is easy access to the reservoir from the town of Sigurd.
Comment: I am not certain if Rocky Ford is actually a place to boat. When we visited, it was drained of water, and there was little to explore. The setting is actually quite nice, and it could be a good spot if the water level increases. The reservoir may or may not be in existence, but what remained could be paddled. I would definitely suggest checking into it.

SCIPIO LAKE
County: Millard
LONG/LAT: N39 07.279 W112 03.307
Size: Approximately 40 acres (varies)
Directions: From Salina, head northwest about 15 miles. The lake is on your left. Take the dirt road turnoff on the north side.
Comment: Low, flat, muddy, and somewhat inaccessible, this may be a difficult spot to paddle. There is a small dirt road that takes you to the lakeshore, but the whole spot feels more like a flooded wetland than an actual lake. The rural setting is quite pretty, and as far as I could tell, access is public.

CHAPTER 8

Book Cliffs are stunning from Cedar Overlook.

Castle Country Region

The Castle Country Region earned its name from the massive sandstone plateaus that decorate its landscape and resemble the ramparts of a castle. These immense flat-topped mountains are beautiful and fascinating. The mixed coloration of the stone displays the geology that has existed in this region since the time of the dinosaurs.

However, just because the region has earned this name does not mean the landscape is exclusively desert plateaus. In fact, some of the most beautiful mountain reservoirs in Utah are a short drive up a

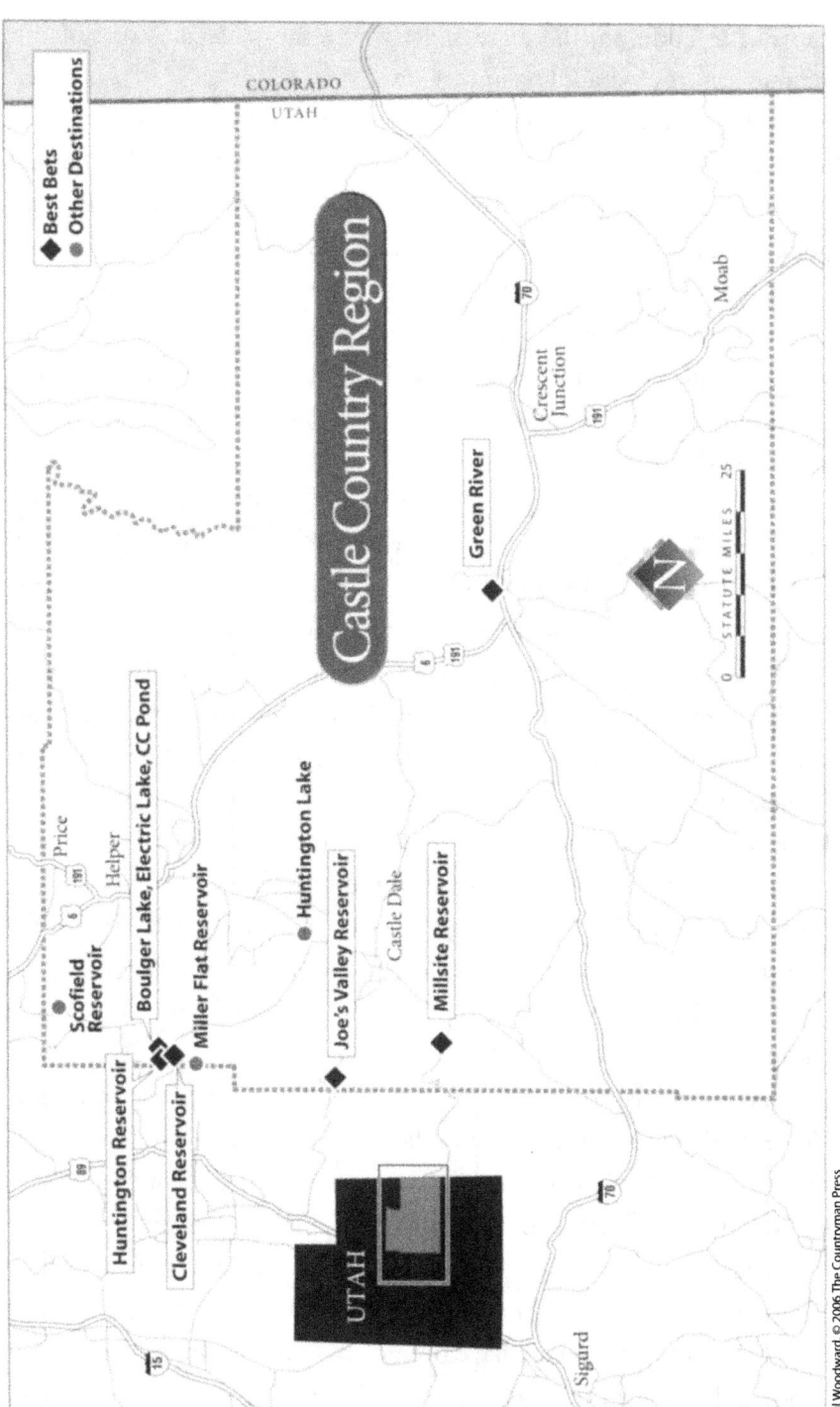

canyon. In addition, there are spots where the plateau is one of the unique features of paddling in this area.

Miles of desert distinguish the Castle Country Region. However, it is also a place of history. Locations in this region are littered with dinosaur remnants and Native American relics and petroglyphs. Veins of coal, gold, and oil are still being pursued and extracted.

Castle Country is about hidden treasures and undiscovered locations. The paddling in this region is no different. There are many spots noted in this section that must be visited. I am certain that when you explore the waters noted here, you too will want to pursue and investigate these discoveries.

An excellent starting point for this pursuit is Price. The largest and most prominent city in the region, Price is a community built by coal mining. The town continues to be supported by the mining industry, and there is an active coal mine just a short drive up Price Canyon.

Price has an excellent museum of paleontology, which has some of the finds from the region. In addition, Price is close to Nine Mile Canyon. This ancient place has been settled for centuries and is considered to have one of the greatest concentrations of petroglyphs in the region. Price is a small community, but a large metropolis for this region.

Huntington is a nearby rural community, founded in 1877. The town was named for the Huntington brothers, who first explored this area. They were scouts and translators who surveyed the area and helped lead to settlements in the region. Huntington remains rooted in its rural background and is not really suited to tourists.

Because of its proximity to Price, the city has very little business. However, the place is pleasant, and there are a couple of sites to see. The road to Cedar Overlook is a lengthy drive on a dirt road. However, at the end you'll find beautiful vistas of book cliffs and plateaus.

Nearby you can find the Cleveland-Lloyd Dinosaur Quarry. Cleveland is one of the most famous and important dinosaur fossil sources in the world. There have been discoveries of more than 12,000 bones and a single dinosaur egg in this location. Though it no longer serves as a quarry, scientists still study it to help understand the geology that made it such a plentiful location for dinosaur bones.

To the east is the San Rafael Swell, a large, isolated, and fascinating geological formation located relatively close to Ferron. With its expansive canyons and abundant petroglyphs, the Swell is an excellent spot for hiking. The history of both our earth and its early people can be tasted with a visit.

One place in the Swell that should not be missed is Goblin Valley State Park. Its large gatherings of mushroom-shaped rock formations are a joy for everyone to explore. These distinct, magical rock shapes have been formed by wind and water erosion. The place feels like an alien landscape and has been used by Hollywood for this purpose.

Grand County is interesting in that there is only one distinctive paddle opportunity, yet it is probably Utah's most famous spot. Labyrinth Canyon and the Green River draw tourists from around the world. The large red-rock canyons and unique setting have an allure for canoeists and kayakers everywhere.

The city of Green River is the primary launching spot for trips down its namesake. There is a state park with a ranger station, where you can get your permits and notify the rangers of your intent to paddle the river. The town is also well known for its watermelons. Every September, Green River celebrates its famous fruit with a festival called Melon Days. Be certain to taste one if you visit.

On your way south, make a stop at Dead Horse Point. There are numerous rumors about how the place got its name. A single visit will inspire your imagination. This massive gorge descends 2,000 feet (610 meters) to the Colorado River. The sheer cliffs and red plateaus are spectacular.

While in the area, you are close to some of Utah's most famous locations. First, Arches National Park makes its home in the county. Millions of years of erosion have created something that should not be missed. The large concentration of arches is something you can't find anywhere else in the world.

Below Arches is the city of Moab. World-renowned home to biking, this small community has thrived in recent years and is now home to many trendy restaurants, art galleries, and shops. The town resides on the Colorado River, and while there is paddling, it is mostly the whitewater type that people are drawn to in this region.

In this open yet isolated region, paddling may not be the first thing people consider when they visit. You can go miles without seeing even the slightest evidence of water. However, as this chapter will show, there are some beautiful, amazing, and often surprising settings.

The landscape transitions from white to red when you move from the northern parts of the region to the southern. From the castlelike plateaus to the smooth red rock, this region holds treasures waiting to be discovered.

BEST BETS

MILLSITE RESERVOIR
County: Emery
LONG/LAT: N39 05.523 W111 11.687
Elevation: 6,212 feet/1,893 meters
Body Type: Reservoir
Difficulty: Easy
Season: Spring, summer, autumn, winter
Size: 435 acres
Directions: From Price, head south on UT 10 to Ferron. Take a right on Ferron Canyon Road. The reservoir is about 2 miles from town.
Put-in: There is a boat ramp within the confines of the state park that is very suitable for launching.
Other Sports: Fishing, camping, bird-watching, hiking, climbing, swimming
Information: www.stateparks.utah.gov/park_pages/parkpage.php?id=mssp

Millsite is a state park with excellent facilities.

Paddle Overview

One of the things that makes paddling in Utah such a joy is the diversity that the state provides. As you climb and descend through its mountains, you watch as the foliage and formations change. Millsite is a perfect example of this mixture. Its massive white cliffs and desert shores are as distinctive as they are beautiful.

Unlike many other lakes I visited, this reservoir exists on a high plateau. The water resides at the base of an even larger highland that is scenic and fascinating. These flat-topped terraces exhibit their layered colored rock softly and gently as they transition into the blue sky.

The water at Millsite is gentle and well protected. It seems to sit in a basin and is completely surrounded by the plateau. While the reservoir is fairly large, it lacks any really interesting paddle features. Round in shape with one small peninsula, the reservoir has few trees, and most of the shore is sandy.

This abundant shoreline lends itself well to portaging and shore paddling. In addition, Millsite is a state park with excellent accommodations for a visit. Nice rest rooms and a good boat launch make it very user friendly.

Powerboaters frequent the reservoir, but on my visit, the water was empty, and we had the place to ourselves. The Millsite area is fairly isolated and unpopulated. In addition, there are numerous other reservoirs that are closer to the more-populated areas of the state.

Millsite is located at the mouth of Ferron Canyon. This is a notable destination for people going into the Manti-La Sal Mountains for fishing and camping. Just before the dam is a stunning golf course with greens and fairways that stand out starkly against the landscape.

Millsite provides a unique paddling backdrop with excellent services. If you are looking for something different from the typical pine-lined lake, Millsite might be the change you imagined. From its white shores to green waters, it is unlike almost any other place I have seen.

GREEN RIVER

County: Grand
LONG/LAT: N38 59.326 W110 09.020 (put-in)
  N38 30.000 W110 01.448 (take-out)
Elevation: 4,079 feet/1,243 meters
Body Type: River
Difficulty: Difficult
Season: Spring, summer, autumn
Size: 68 miles
Directions: Green River State Park is located just off I-70 in Green River, via the business loop. Signs for the park are clearly marked. There is access to Mineral Bottom via UT 313 north of Moab.

Before the junction of Dead Horse Point State Park and Canyonlands National Park, a small sign marks the turnoff to Mineral Bottom. This is a dirt road that can become dangerous in wet conditions.

Put-in: Within the confines of the state park, there is a boat ramp that is very suitable for launching.

Other Sports: Fishing, camping, bird-watching, hiking, climbing, swimming

Information: www.blm.gov/utah/price/labyrinth.htm; 435-636-3600

Paddle Overview

There are few paddles that are more famous or desired than the trek from Green River State Park to Mineral Bottom. This stretch of the Green has been immortalized in photography, film, and paddling lore.

Sunset over the Green River

The scenery and slow-moving river draw people from around the globe to experience this distinctive paddle.

While this book is focused on providing detailed information about paddle destinations in the various regions, this particular trip consumes entire books, and there are innumerable guides published to assist you with this 68-mile trip. However, it would be neglectful of me not to take the time to mention this important destination and discuss the various aspects of this paddle.

The Green River is one of this country's most distinctive rivers. It is an oasis that has provided the lifeblood to some of the most desolate places in the American West. The Green changes significantly as it treks south through Utah. From its release at the Flaming Gorge Dam to its confluence with the Colorado River, it carves a path of heritage and history.

There are two common put-ins. The first put-in point for the trip is at Green River State Park. The second is at Crystal Geyser. The usual take-out is at Mineral Bottom, where a ranger is on duty most of the time from mid-March through October. This long journey takes anywhere from three to six days, depending on your speed and the amount of supplies you can tote.

The journey that unfolds as you descend the river is something of legends. Labyrinth Canyon is defined by its massive walls and stunning red-rock cliffs. The paddle is quite unique as you gently float down the river that created these epic canyons.

The murky brown water of the Green is smooth and calm throughout the journey. Even in the spring when the river is high, there is little concern for the most novice paddler. However, the journey is long, and someone without paddling experience might be overwhelmed.

Along its shores you will find muddy embankments decorated by small bushes, shrubs, and trees. In this desolate desert, life teems in the canyon. Throughout its history, the river has served as an oasis for both animals and humans alike. In fact, evidence of this can be seen along the way, with Native American petroglyphs and the etchings of visitors from long ago.

Many people prefer to spend more time on their journey by taking one of the many hikes along the river. These trails are accessible only by boat and allow you to climb up a number of the noted canyons and formations.

If you plan on taking this trip, you will need to make many special preparations. Transportation, permits, and proper gear need to be put in order before you can embark. The Bureau of Land Management concerns itself with maintaining the historic and natural setting of the canyon and has very specific rules about floating.

Beyond paddling, the object of this trip is retaining the natural qualities of the environment by leaving no trace. This is one of the few remaining wilderness rivers left in the country, and you should expect to practice conservation. It is your obligation to help retain the beauty of the Green as it was when John Wesley Powell first explored it back in 1869.

The Green River is certainly one of the finest rivers in the state and a paddling destination that everyone should make. Floating such a beautiful and historic location is without comparison and has to be experienced to truly appreciate it.

JOE'S VALLEY RESERVOIR

County: Emery
LONG/LAT: N39 18.051 W111 16.332
Elevation: 6,996 feet/2,132 meters
Body Type: Reservoir
Difficulty: Moderate
Season: Spring, summer, autumn
Size: 1,183 acres
Directions: From Price, travel south on UT 10 for 22 miles to Huntington. From Huntington, continue south on UT 10 for 6 miles to a sign on your right pointing the way to Joe's Valley and UT 29. You will pass through Orangeville and come to a T-intersection in the road. Follow the road to the right, up Straight Canyon to the top.

An old mine cart near Joe's Valley Reservoir

Put-in: There is an excellent boat ramp and brand-new parking lot on the east side of the reservoir. There is also a professional marina on the water as well. If neither of these suit you, there are large areas of sandy shoreline.

Other Sports: Fishing, camping, hiking, climbing

Information: www.castlecountry.com/what_to_see/joes_valley.html

Paddle Overview

Joe's Valley feels like a secret that I should be reluctant to share. Trekking through a canyon decorated with massive boulders and a raging river, you suddenly come to a beautiful valley with a large reservoir beckoning to be paddled. Joe's Valley is a little spot of heaven.

A large reservoir, it is relatively isolated from other bodies of water. This is part of its allure. The winding drive up the canyon into the valley is a subtle transition from the buttes and plateaus in the west to distinctive mountains. You feel like you are being transported to a special place.

Once the valley unfolds in front you, the road turns to the north and winds its way around the reservoir. You'll see that the area is oblong with steep rugged mountain terrain on the east and more gentle slopes on the west. In either direction, the views are delightful.

The reservoir covers the entire valley floor. Its shoreline varies from rocky shoals to sandy beaches. Large boulders can be seen on the mountainside and along the water. In other areas, trees cast shadows across the water and shelter small coves along the steep, mountainous coastline. It is an exquisite site that invites paddling and camping.

The water is a touch cool at this altitude, but it is clear, clean, and blue. This is yet another way Joe's Valley evokes a forgotten place. While it is a popular destination, it still has that hidden charm. You do not see evidence of the crowds. The place feels pristine and untouched.

One thing that indicates use is the excellent facilities. There is a marina, new rest rooms, and a great boat launch. In addition, there are multiple campgrounds available at the lake, but there is a fee if you plan to make an overnight stay. In addition, there are convenient hiking paths and some picnic areas.

If you are looking for a large paddle area that feels private, Joe's Valley will certainly do the trick. Take the long drive up from Castledale past Cottonwood Creek to this special place. When you get there, tell them Joe sent you.

BOULGER LAKE, ELECTRIC LAKE, CC POND

County: Emery
LONG/LAT: Boulger N39 38.688 W111 15.254
   Electric N39 38.259 W111 14.187
   CC Pond N39 39.307 W111 17.787
Elevation: 8,600 feet (average)/2,621 meters (average)

Body Type: Lakes and a reservoir
Difficulty: Easy
Season: Summer
Size: Boulger approximately 15 acres
Electric 425 acres
CC Pond approximately 10 acres
Directions: From Price, head northwest on US 6/191 up the canyon. Just past Colton, take a left on UT 96. Follow UT 96 around Scofield Reservoir and continue to UT 264. Take a right on UT 264 to all three lakes.
Put-in: For Boulger, there is a short pier right off the parking area that is easy to use as a put-in. For CC Pond, there is a variety of easy put-ins, but you can simply park on the small dam and drop in your boat. Electric has a very long boat ramp.
Other Sports: Fishing, camping
Information: None

Paddle Overview

When making selections for the best the region had to offer, these three lakes could not stand on their own. Electric is massive, narrow, and daunting; the other two are small and not exceptionally good places to paddle. However, you can combine this triad of lakes, located in the Wasatch Plateau, for a single interesting excursion.

For those who want a challenging paddle, Electric is situated in a long canyon with steep walls and a narrow passage. There are few places you can find a reservoir that has such a unique shape. The north end is very narrow, and the lake gradually widens until it reaches the dam. However, it never quite reaches a triangular shape. The width increases only slightly with the introduction of a few smaller canyons.

Electric has no decent shore or beach to stop on once you begin your trek to the dam. In addition, the water is very deep and cold. Depending on the water level, you may have committed yourself to paddling until

The boardwalk at CC Pond

you decide to return. At the far end, two interesting structures in the water are visible if you come through Huntington Canyon.

If something lighter is your taste, try Boulger and CC Pond. These two small natural lakes are marshy and might be too small to make a real effort to paddle. However, they are beautiful and have nice facilities and easy access. The pine-decorated mountainsides and lovely green valleys make a delightful setting for time on the water.

The marshy shorelines are a touch muddy, but both lakes provide solid access. There is some exposure, but for the most part, the wind should not be an issue. CC and Boulger are around the corner from one another and very close to the massive Electric Lake. These lakes also provide fantastic fishing. On my visits, the fish were literally jumping out of the water. Even if you never fished a day in your life, I imagine you will be able to catch something.

In all, I don't know if I would bring a boat exclusively to paddle either of these little lakes, but they are nice spots on the way to many other beautiful destinations. If you plan a trip to Electric, a small kayak or canoe would do well in either of these sister lakes.

The most distinctive aspects of these lakes are CC's boardwalks and Boulger's pier. These places were designed with handicap accessibility in mind. Each small body of water provides a nice place for fishing or shoreline access for those in wheelchairs. Its accessibility means that everyone can enjoy these special spots.

I also noted rest rooms at each location and some very nice camping by Boulger. The camping spots are perfect because Boulger sits in between Electric and CC. Use this ideal spot as a jumping off point for visits to the other two.

Coming up from either Price Canyon or through Huntington, you will discover that this is coal mining country. In either direction you will see that coal has played a critical part of the history of the region, and it remains an important part of the economy today. Keep a close eye on the rock formations that line the canyons as you drive. In some of the rock, you can see lines of coal.

These three bodies of water are very different from one another, but really compliment each other. Electric is the big boy offering challenge and an interesting landscape. Boulger is a marshy paddle with an interesting shoreline, and CC is the perfect fishing hole. On this visit, there is paddling for the whole family.

CLEVELAND RESERVOIR
County: Emery
LONG/LAT: N39 34.928 W111 14.780
Elevation: 8,823 feet/2,689 meters
Body Type: Reservoir
Difficulty: Easy
Season: Summer

The abundant beach at Cleveland Reservoir

Size: 185 acres

Directions: From Huntington, take UT 31 northwest approximately 30 miles. The lake appears on your left, directly off the road. The parking area is on the west side of the road.

Put-in: The shoreline is very accessible. You can drive right down in some areas. Put in close to the parking-lot level if the water is high enough.

Other Sports: Fishing, camping, hiking

Information: None

Paddle Overview

As you head up Huntington Canyon to Cleveland Reservoir, you pass staggeringly beautiful and shaded campsites next to a river. The canyon walls climb upward, casting a slight shadow over the valley. This darkening has an interesting effect, because the green becomes almost luminescent. As you ascend, the colors fade and change to an entirely different landscape.

The 3,000-foot ascent from Huntington to Cleveland is barely noticeable. Your eye is drawn to the surroundings, and the time passes quickly. Before you realize how far you have traveled, you are at Cleveland. The reward for this drive is one of the more stunning paddle locations available in this canyon.

The most significant benefit of Cleveland is its abundant beach. It makes for an easy portage. Most of the shoreline is sandy or slightly rocky and very accessible. I was able to drive right up to the shore in my Outback. You will find many put-ins right off the road or from the small west-side parking lot.

The water at the reservoir is cold, but appears to be well protected from the influence of wind. The surrounding mountains and dam should provide protection from the wind and allow the reservoir to maintain a smooth surface in most conditions.

This protection is also what makes Cleveland so scenic. Tall pines, delicate aspens, and mountain vistas are the setting for this reservoir. You will find its setting relaxing and its size very manageable. While it is rather featureless, it is a nice place for shore paddling.

The reservoir resides at nearly 9,000 feet, so it can get cool even during the summer months. However, this is a benefit, because the lower Castle Country Region is notably hot during the summer months. Cleveland is an excellent escape from the temperatures.

You might find Cleveland primitive, but this is part of its appeal. If you opt to camp at the reservoir, you will have to pack out your own garbage because there are no facilities available. However, I would avoid camping here and grab a spot in one of the many locations in the canyon.

HUNTINGTON RESERVOIR (MAMMOTH RESERVOIR)

County: Sanpete
LONG/LAT: N39 35.176 W111 15.630
Elevation: 8,957 feet/2,730 meters
Body Type: Reservoir
Difficulty: Easy
Season: Summer
Size: 118 acres
Directions: From Huntington, take UT 31 northwest approximately 32 miles. The lake appears on your left, directly off the road. There is parking on the south end of the reservoir near the dam.
Put-in: Just off the dam is a convenient shore area ideal for a put-in.
Other Sports: Fishing, camping, bird-watching, hiking, climbing, swimming
Information: None

Paddle Overview

There can be some confusion because Huntington shares its name with another large body of water in central Utah. However, the similarities end there. Where Huntington *Lake* is a desert oasis, the Huntington *Reservoir* is a beautiful mountain locale with soaring pines in a fertile, green setting.

The reservoir, located on the Wasatch Plateau, is elongated and has a large dam on the south end. It is positioned just off the road, and its shore is easily accessible from the small parking lot located in the same area. This tree-lined reservoir has a lot of shore available, depending on water levels and your ability to access it from the road.

Huntington gained some fame back in the 1980s when modernization on the dam revealed the skeletal remains of a nearly 11,000-year-old wooly mammoth. At the time, discoveries at the high elevations of the reservoir were rare. They suggest that the mammoth was trapped in a bog and died in the location just prior to the extinction of its kind. You can view the casts of the bones at the paleontology museum in Price.

Paddlers are drawn to trek the length of Huntington Reservoir.

While the area has lost much of its prehistoric charm, it retains the qualities that we desire in a good paddle. The reservoir is surrounded by lofty mountain crests, which provide excellent protection from the wind.

Huntington has a long shape and sufficient surface area to make it a decent challenge. Paddlers are naturally drawn to make a trek lengthwise and return. Though the reservoir is not of significant size, there is more than enough paddle here for a morning or afternoon on the water.

Huntington is a good-quality location with very easy access. It provides lovely scenery and a gentle surface to paddle. However, take caution. The one thing this reservoir teaches us is to be careful paddling in marshy or boggy areas. I don't think anyone wants to turn up 11,000 years late for dinner.

OTHER DESTINATIONS

HUNTINGTON LAKE
County: Emery
LONG/LAT: N39 20.712 W110 56.425
Size: 237 acres
Directions: From Price, take UT 10 south to Huntington. The reservoir is located to the left just before you enter the city.
Comment: Huntington Lake is very congenial, but there are few interesting aspects. It is not significantly large, and its round shape makes it a standard destination. In addition, it is not an ideal spot for paddling because it is frequented by powerboats. For a more interesting experience, put in a little extra drive time up Huntington Canyon and enjoy some beautiful mountain lakes.

SCOFIELD RESERVOIR
County: Carbon
LONG/LAT: N39 44.982 W111 09.052
Size: 2,800 acres
Directions: From Price, take US 6 northwest up Price Canyon. Take a left onto UT 96, and follow the road to the state park. The roads are well marked, and there are many spots to put in.
Comment: Scofield is very large and very popular. There are valid reasons for this. The large surface area, great lake facilities, and close proximity to Price and Utah County attract people on both sides of the mountains. However, boat traffic means this might not be an ideal spot for paddling.

MILLER FLAT RESERVOIR

County: Emery

LONG/LAT: N39 34.522 W111 15.386

Size: 160 acres

Directions: From Huntington, take UT 31 northwest approximately 31 miles. There is a dirt road halfway between Cleveland and Huntington. Make the left and drive about 4 miles south to the reservoir.

Comment: This is a beautiful spot; if you don't mind a bumpy dirt road, it is worth the visit. However, I find Cleveland and Huntington to be equal to it in beauty.

Part of the amazing landscape that is the Red Rock Region

Red Rock Region

When I first moved to Utah, many people I knew raved of the beauty and the sense of exhilaration that the state's southern landscape provided. Friends of mine drove miles to get wedding pictures and family photos and to vacation in what I considered a bunch of rocks.

I questioned their enthusiasm. With the amazing skiing, beautiful green mountains, and high alpine lakes of the north, I could not imagine the appeal this hot and isolated terrain could hold. Yet a single visit is all it takes to become captivated by this enchanting place. The scenery in this part of the state is unparalleled; no matter how much I try to

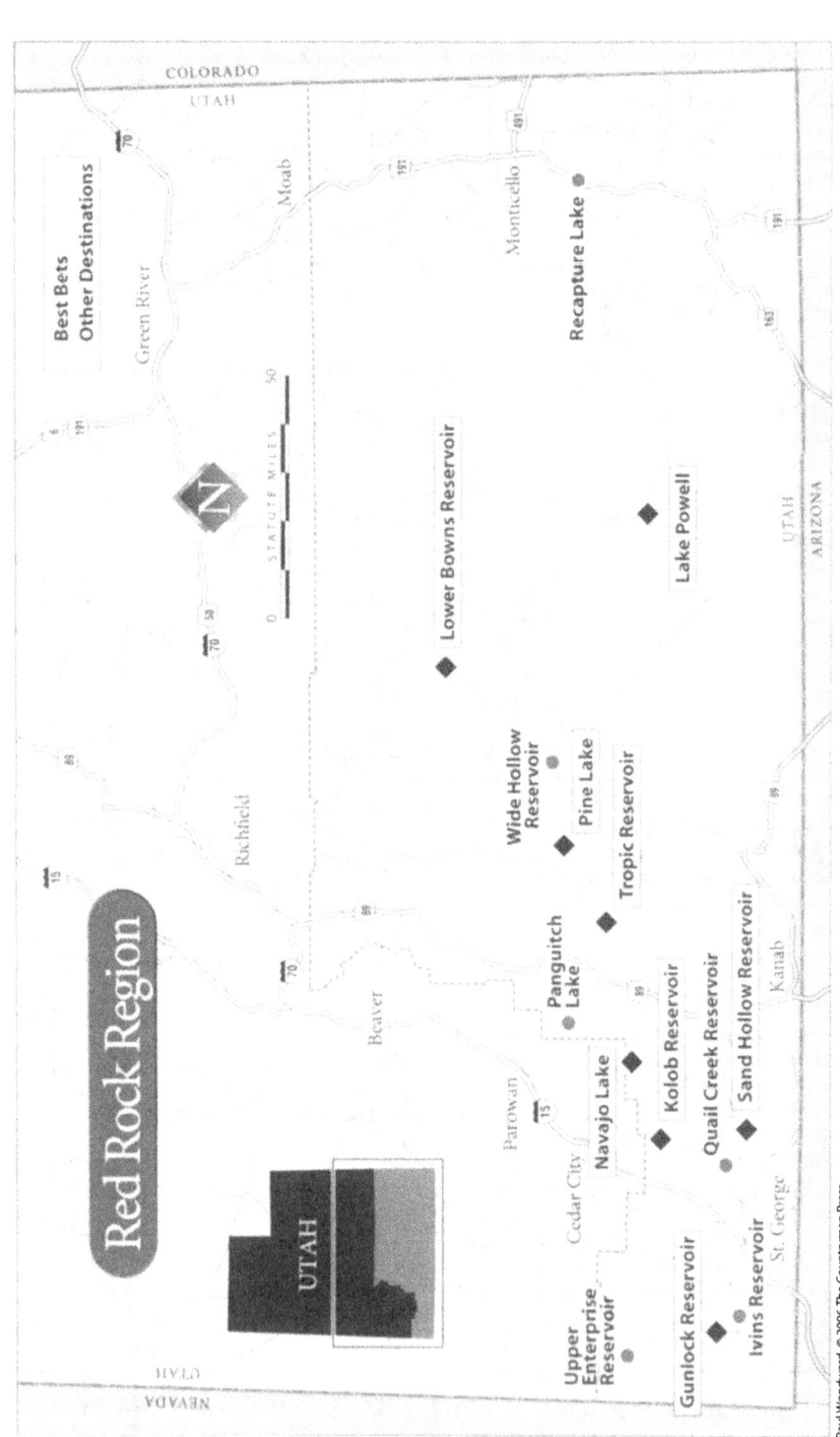

convey here, it can't express the unequalled beauty of these places—from the towering red spires of Bryce to the plateaus of Capitol Reef.

The state's vacationland, this southern area is called Utah's Dixie. Early pioneers attempted to develop a cotton industry in the region. St. George, the largest city in the region, is a thriving metropolis with a charming, historic downtown and abundant golf courses.

Surrounding St. George you have the small communities of Washington, Hurricane, Santa Clara, and Ivins. At one time, these small towns stood alone as separate places. However, the continual sprawl in the region has brought these once-isolated towns together. It is now a bit harder to distinguish where one ends and another begins.

This growth did not bury the history or the identities of these towns; along your way, take some time to explore the many fascinating historical sites and other unique locations. In Santa Clara, you have a grand view of the Red Mountains; nearby Ivins is home to Tuacahn, an outdoor professional theater that resides in a canyon with 1,500-foot cliffs; and Hurricane is a city with strong agricultural heritage.

Farther east you have Zion National Park. This amazing place is unlike any other in the world. Rather than view the majesty of a canyon from its rim, Zion gives you a chance to see it from the base. These towering vertical walls climb thousands of feet in the air, providing an excellent perspective on the relatively diminutive size of humans.

Zion has many fascinating hikes and wonderful geological displays to explore. One of the more popular attractions is the Narrows. This 12.5-mile trek takes you up the Virgin River through a canyon that often shrinks to a point where you can touch both sides at once. The water usually is ankle deep, but some parts can be above your head, depending on the time of the year.

Just outside Zion is the delightful little town of Springdale. This community is the western gateway to the park and focuses on providing an interesting and artsy experience. Galleries, shopping, and restaurants vie for your attention as you make your way into the park.

Farther north you will find the charming city of Panguitch. This small community, nestled in the center of the Dixie National Forest, has a real feeling of Americana, complete with the traditional main street. This town is an excellent jumping-off point to many of the paddling destinations noted in this region.

Another interesting spot in the region is the small town of Boulder. A charming little art community with several restaurants and galleries, it is a perfect place to stay if you are exploring the Red Rock Region. Nearby are the famed ruins of the Anasazi. These Native Americans disappeared almost a thousand years ago, but their cliff dwellings remain.

Boulder is also close to many of the slot canyons that were created by millions of years of erosion from wind and rain. These narrow canyons display Mother Nature's finest work with undulating curves and amazing aesthetics. Because of the harsh nature of this wilderness, be certain to do some research before exploring these canyons.

Until as recently as the 1930s, Boulder was only accessible by pack mule. Now you can drive from Boulder to Escalante on the Million Dollar Road. Not for anyone with vertigo, this road connects the two cities and allows you to drive through the Grand Staircase Escalante National Monument. A winding cliff path, with steep grades and stunning views, takes you through the monument.

The Grand Staircase Escalante National Monument is an immense area of tall cliffs, plateaus, river valleys, and canyons. The monument is a virtual paradise for geologists, hikers, and backpackers. It was once a home to the Anasazi and Fremont tribes, and remnants of these civilizations can be found throughout the monument.

On the opposite side of the monument, Glen Canyon and world-renowned Lake Powell reside. With more than 100 miles of surface area, this lake was formed when a dam was created at the mouth of Glen Canyon to block the mighty Colorado River. Utah's most noted marina is at Bullfrog, where paddlers and powerboaters depart for canyon excursions.

Throughout the Red Rock Region, there are ample accommodations. The region is accustomed to tourism and welcomes visitors from around the globe. You will often find a friendly face no matter where you choose to visit. Those who have made their home in this region have been enchanted by their surroundings as well.

BEST BETS

KOLOB RESERVOIR
County: Washington
LONG/LAT: N37 26.295 W113 02.693
Elevation: 7,993 feet/2,436 meters
Body Type: Reservoir
Difficulty: Moderate
Season: Spring, summer, autumn
Size: 249 acres
Directions: From St. George, take I-15 north to exit 15. Head east on UT 9 through Hurricane and Virgin. Just past Virgin, take a left onto Kolob Reservoir Road. Follow it until you get to the reservoir. It is about 25 miles.
Put-in: There are two boat ramps and abundant shore locations where you can put in your boat.
Other Sports: Fishing, camping, bird-watching, hiking, climbing
Information: www.americansouthwest.net/utah/zion/kolob_reservoir.html

Paddle Overview
There are moments when paddling becomes poetry. The drive, the put-in, the paddle, the conditions, and the experience come together into a single perfect experience. Of all the destinations I visited in my pursuit to complete this book, Kolob is one of the few that meets every criteria for a perfect paddle. It has everything you can imagine, and then it only gets better. It is a piece of poetry just waiting to be paddled.

For starters, the drive is simply stunning. The road to Kolob treks through a portion of Zion National Park that most people probably miss. The impressive red rock formations rival those inside the main areas of the park. The drive alone is worth the visit.

Along the way, there are numerous trailheads that take you to some of Zion's notable rock formations. Until you get close to the reservoir, you will be constantly surprised by the transforming landscape. The drive to the reservoir can be quite long if you continually stop to catch the many striking views.

Once you arrive at the reservoir, your put-in is simple. The road winds along the perimeter of the reservoir, and there is more shore than necessary to drop a boat into the water. In addition, there are two boat ramps on the east side of the reservoir. One is on the south end, and the other on the north.

Immediately you realize that this is a very fascinating paddle. There are islands, inlets, and other unique features to pursue by canoe or kayak. The shape of the reservoir is very interesting and should provide hours of paddling exploration.

Around the lake, small rolling mountains provide nice shelter and lovely scenery. Throngs of quaking aspens are complimented by the occasional patch of pine and other evergreen trees. Nearby there are numerous grassy fields and subtle rock formations that will add to the camping or picnicking experience.

Powerboats are allowed on the reservoir, but they are not really an issue because most are just fishing. There are more convenient and suitable places for speed closer to the population centers. Kolob is much too high and too small to be appealing to water-skiers or personal-watercraft users.

If you plan to stay the night, there are many excellent shore-camping spots located around the reservoir. However, if you're interested in staying in a hotel or bed-and-breakfast, there are many nearby. Kolob is in an excellent location. It sits just a short drive from Springdale, Virgin, and Hurricane.

Paddling alongside piñon and juniper

The scenery around Kolob is simply amazing. The massive red rock formations that Utah is famous for are everywhere. While there are no notable formations at the reservoir, you pass through Zion and can revel in its beauty. Perhaps it is better that way, because with every good poem, its message is subtle.

LOWER BOWNS RESERVOIR (BOWNS RESERVOIR, BOUNDS RESERVOIR)
County: Garfield
LONG/LAT: N38 06.330 W111 16.562
Elevation: 7,434 feet/2,266 meters
Body Type: Reservoir
Difficulty: Easy
Season: Spring, summer, autumn

Size: 90 acres

Directions: From Boulder, head north on UT 12 for about 19 miles. There is a forest-service dirt road on the right. Take it for about 5 miles. It ends at the dam. There are good signs from UT 12.

Put-in: There are a lot of shoreline camp spots that are adequate for a put-in. You may find some muddy spots, depending on the weather.

Other Sports: Fishing, camping, hiking

Information: None

Paddle Overview

The first time I saw the name of this reservoir, I thought it was a typo. Bowns seemed like a strange name for a place, and I kept finding myself swapping the *D* for the *B*. I tried to discover the source of the name for this book, but discovered only that I was not alone in my confusion. While the name might be difficult, the paddling is a delight.

Located on the east flank of Boulder Mountain, Lower Bowns is a reservoir that borders the western edge of Capitol Reef National Park. As you descend to the reservoir, ancient geological formations can be seen in the distance, and the location is rich in color. The park is known for its colorful stone, and Lower Bowns contrasts beautifully to its surroundings.

This smaller-sized reservoir is nestled deep in the desert surroundings. The sandy shores are ideal for putting in, and the water is cool and pleasant during the heat of the summer. The reservoir sits in a recessed plot; when I was out on a fairly windy day, the rock cliffs provided excellent cover. The piñon and juniper also create a protective embrace.

The road to Lower Bowns is not exactly ideal. It is a bit rough in spots; while it is maintained, weather and use have created a rut-ridden surface. But the drive is not too long and is worth taking to get to the reservoir.

The put-in is simple because there is great, easy access along the shore. I did manage to find a few muddy spots, and there is a marshy aspect to the western side. Yet you can still drive right up to the reservoir and drop your boat in for a float. This is especially nice if you plan to camp at the site.

We saw a number of people fishing and discovered that the place is quite popular. On your visit, be certain to drive to the top of the dam and look to the west at the small stream burrowing its way through the desert soil. This beautiful little spot was fascinating to watch.

On your way out, take a moment to head north up UT 12 and get a view from the Larb Hollow Overlook. This point provides an excellent view of the Water Pocket Hollow of Capitol Reef, as well as the reservoir. Lower Bowns looks beautiful from this spot, its blue water startling against the red rock. Perhaps seeing it from here will help you remember its name.

TROPIC RESERVOIR

County: Garfield
LONG/LAT: N37 36.256 W112 15.373
Elevation: 7,836 feet/2,388 meters
Body Type: Reservoir
Difficulty: Moderate
Season: Spring, summer, autumn
Size: 180 acres
Directions: From Panguitch, follow UT 12 through Red Canyon toward Bryce. On your right, about 8 miles from Red Canyon, you will find a good dirt road called East Fork of the Sevier River Scenic Backway. Follow the road south for about 8 miles. The reservoir is on the right.
Put-in: There are some campsites with shore access, and on the west side you can find a road relatively close. On the east side, midway to the top, there is a small inlet that could work well, but has a steep portage to the water.
Other Sports: Fishing, camping, hiking
Information: www.recreation.gov/detail.cfm?ID=1195

The breathtaking formations of Red Canyon

Paddle Overview

There is little I can say about Tropic Reservoir that can adequately describe it. This matchless location provides wonderful paddling and a beautiful setting. However, it is more than this. Tropic is sort of like a paraphrase of Utah's southern landscape. Deep red rocks, evergreen forest, mountains, and interspersed sandstone create a unique spot to paddle.

Located near Bryce Canyon National Park on the Colorado Plateau, the reservoir shares some of the same formations as its distinguished neighbor. Tall spires interrupt the mountain landscape only a short distance from the reservoir. In addition, Tropic's blend of emerald forest, crimson pillars, and cerulean sky is intoxicating.

The north end is where the water is deepest and most easily paddled. Close to the dam, you will find the most dramatic scenery and the easiest access to the water. However, there is some interesting paddling on the south side. This part is much shallower and marshy. The East Fork of the Sevier River flows through this area into the reservoir throughout the year, but snowmelt makes the flow stronger in the spring.

The south end of the reservoir also has some fascinating erosion that has taken the form of mounds. The small hills are completely surrounded by water; they may be islands in the spring and then turn into muddy mounds as irrigation drains the reservoir. Depending on the water depth and time of the year, these unique features are fun to explore.

Mountains on the north end seem to protect you from excessive winds; because of the high embankment around the entire reservoir, it is unlikely that you will find much impact from the wind. Add the fact that this region has very little precipitation in the summer months, and you should find Tropic a pleasant float whenever you choose to visit.

One of the side benefits of visiting Tropic is the opportunity to drive UT 12, which is probably one of the best drives in the state. Traversing across the Grand Staircase, Red Canyon, and many other natural and historical sites, this amazing drive happens to have some access to stellar paddling.

Paddling is not always the thought when people make their trek down to this area. The abundant hiking, camping, and biking seem to overwhelm any thoughts of a good paddle. However, Tropic is reason enough to bring your kayak or canoe on this trip.

PINE LAKE

County: Garfield
LONG/LAT: N37 44.587 W111 57.406
Elevation: 8,103 feet/2,470 meters
Body Type: Lake
Difficulty: Easy

A charming street in Panguitch

Season: Summer

Size: 77 acres

Directions: From Panguitch, head south on US 89 to the junction of UT 12. Take UT 12 east to UT 22. Take a left on UT 22 and head north about 11 miles. Take a right on Pine Lake Road. There are about three signs indicating where to turn. Follow the road to the lake.

Put-in: There is a perfect spot for a put-in right in the first parking lot before the dam.

Other Sports: Fishing, camping, hiking

Information: None

Paddle Overview

This is a place that feels as if giants in an ancient fortress are defending it. Tree-covered plateaus stand firm to resist entry. You make your way through a narrow passage as a river and daunting pines stand guard. Just before the entrance, the path takes a deeper and darker turn and suddenly expands and opens to your treasure. Pine Lake is here in the heart of the fortress.

As I drove up the windy road to Pine, I never anticipated that this little spot was going to be such a delightful location. The spot is completely isolated, and its bland name does not convey much about it. Yes, there are plentiful pines and it is certainly a lake, but it is much more.

The lake is located on the Table Cliff Plateau, where white stone faces surround and protect you and provide a wonderful setting for paddling. There is more than ample coverage to keep wind from being a factor. The lake has a nice spot at the bottom of this little recess in the plateau, and it looks comfortable.

There are a couple of small, marshy islands located to the east, and while they look stable, I would not explore them unless you want to get wet. Instead, stay in your boat and take in all of the lovely scenery. The rock faces, with their white and red stone, are something to behold.

Pine will not take long to paddle, but you can camp at the lake. It appears as if some money was invested in the area. There were new rest rooms and picnic tables in the area. Also, the road leading up to the lake had multiple appealing campsites.

Pine is certainly a remote lake, and I wonder if those who named it intended to mislead people. This simple and humble name might lead you to believe that it was a dull and typical location. However, it is quite the contrary. Pine is a sublime and subtle spot that deserves your time. You certainly will feel like you have found a rare and precious treasure. However, rather than keep it for yourself, you should share it with your friends and family. There is more than enough of this beautiful lake to go around.

LAKE POWELL

County: San Juan, Kane, Garfield
LONG/LAT: N37 30.970 W110 43.680
Elevation: 3,700 feet/1,128 meters
Body Type: Reservoir
Difficulty: Difficult
Season: Spring, summer, autumn, winter
Size: 167,700 acres
Directions: From Hanksville, take UT 95 south until you reach Hite. Turn right about 1 mile past the Hite Crossing Bridge. For Bullfrog, follow UT 276 to the right and head south. The road ends in Bullfrog. There is a ferry at Bullfrog/Hall's Crossing.
Put-in: There are two predominant marinas to use as put-ins. Hite and Bullfrog both have services, camping, and parking.
Other Sports: Fishing, camping, hiking
Information: www.nps.gov/glca

Paddle Overview

We can't measure the uniqueness of a place solely on its distinctive characteristics. Many places are unique because of simple things that differentiate them from others. However, there is one paddle destination in Utah that stands alone. This is Lake Powell.

Lake Powell is a massive, sprawling body of water that evolved from the creation of a dam on the Colorado River. Unlike other lakes that were created by dams, this lake fills more than one hundred different canyons that descend into tiny spots ideal for paddlers. The red sandstone and barren landscape combine to make this lake one of the world's most fascinating spots.

Lake Powell stretches from the confluence of the Colorado and Dirty Devil rivers down into Arizona just above the Grand Canyon. However, a vast majority of the lake is located in Utah. Its fingered canyons expand in every direction, making the paddling options endless. However, this lake is not simply one you can jump into and paddle.

Exploring the isolated Navajo sandstone canyons at Lake Powell

Trips to Lake Powell require extensive planning. You should expect to spend a few days if you anticipate seeing anything beyond the small bays that are accessible on the Utah side of the lake. This planning must include the ability to pack in and take out everything you need. There are few services available on the lake.

Water conditions on the lake's high-desert landscape are generally very favorable for paddling. During the summer months, it is warm, comfortable, and perfect for swimming. However, the winter brings cooler temperatures to the desert region, and a wetsuit is a requirement if you plan to paddle during this time.

There are two approaches to paddling the lake. The first is the more traditional put-in and paddle motif. This can be done from Bullfrog or Hite. Bullfrog is much more popular and has a lot more to offer in the way of facilities. The second method is to paddle from a houseboat. Many people tow their kayaks and canoes with them so they can get to the farthest reaches of the lake.

Both trips are fantastic opportunities to see some of these isolated Navajo sandstone canyons, which remain untouched by many and provide unique and enriching experiences. In fact, there are numerous sites that can't be accessed by anything but boat.

The chance to explore Lake Powell by boat provides a feeling of exclusivity. From Anasazi ruins to geological features, the lake's features used to be inaccessible to anyone but hikers. With the creation of the lake in the 1960s, many historical, geological, and cultural spots were lost forever. However, something new and unique was created that many now enjoy.

Lake Powell certainly has one of the best backdrops in the state to explore through paddling. Its scenery, climate, and water make it a suitable locale to visit throughout the year. You will not only be able to explore its beauty through paddling, but you will also be able to experience a place that is like nowhere else.

NAVAJO LAKE

County: Kane
LONG/LAT: N37 31.048 W112 45.670
Elevation: 8,995 feet/2,742 meters
Body Type: Lake
Difficulty: Easy
Season: Spring, summer, autumn
Size: 714 acres
Directions: From Panguitch, take US 89 south to UT 14. Follow UT 14 west about 23 miles. Navajo is located on the left. Campgrounds are first, and then the lodge is at the western end.
Put-in: There are numerous campgrounds and shore put-ins.
Other Sports: Fishing, camping, bird-watching, hiking, climbing, swimming
Information: www.utahoutdooractivities.com/navajolake.html
www.navajolakelodge.com

Paddle Overview

It is hard for me to be objective about Navajo Lake. Long before I made my home in Utah, my grandfather owned and operated the lodge at the lake. In the years before he passed away, I made trips down to meet him. We fished together, and he shared his experiences of owning the lodge on this enchanting lake.

More than ten years has passed, and I still have a deep fondness for Navajo. The beautiful place is a natural lake in a perfect alpine setting. It is everything a paddler could desire. Tree-lined shores, clear water, and delicate scenery combine into a recipe for a perfect day on the water.

Navajo Lake is a stunning blue color that your eyes can hardly fathom. In order to appreciate the beauty of this place, you need to make two stops. The first is the scenic overlook on UT 14, which provides a great vista and shows Navajo's large size. The second stop is down on the lake's shore, where you can take in its glassy surface.

A stunning view of Cedar Breaks above Cedar City

The lodge was around long before my grandfather owned it and still provides rustic cabin rentals. These charming little buildings provide all the accommodations necessary for a fun visit at the lake. The cabins do not have refrigerators, but they provide every other accommodation. The lodge rents canoes and aluminum fishing boats.

The water surface at Navajo Lake is long and well protected. The surrounding mountains provide excellent protection from wind, and on most visits you will find a smooth surface to explore. The dense forest that surrounds the lake also provides excellent cover for camping.

It is a very short jaunt from the lake to Cedar Breaks National Monument. This stunning natural amphitheater has an overlook that demonstrates the amazing color contrasts this rock can have, from deep reds to subtle oranges to icy whites. These rock fins extend outward and downward for more than 2,000 feet.

In contrast, Navajo Lake is not distinguished by any unique features. In fact, this is what makes it such a great place. It is simply a template for the perfect mountain getaway. Its high altitude, grand scenery, and wonderful water conditions make it an ideal spot to bring the family for a paddle vacation.

SAND HOLLOW RESERVOIR

County: Washington
LONG/LAT: N37 07.136 W113 23.006
Elevation: 3,023 feet/921 meters
Body Type: Reservoir
Difficulty: Easy
Season: Spring, summer, autumn, winter
Size: 1,000 acres
Directions: From St. George, head north on I-15. Take exit 16 (UT 9) and travel east for 2 miles. Turn left on Turf Sod Road, travel 1 mile, and turn left on Sand Hollow Road for 2 miles. Turn left into the entrance to the park.
Put-in: There is an excellent boat ramp just inside the entrance of the park.
Other Sports: Camping, swimming
Information: www.utah.com/stateparks/sand_hollow.htm

Paddle Overview
If you can't make the trek all the way to Lake Powell, a visit to Sand Hollow State Park may satiate the need to paddle among the red rocks. Located just west of Hurricane, this new reservoir has an interesting setting and some fun features to explore by canoe or kayak.

Paddling at the state's new recreation area, Sand Hollow State Park

Sand Hollow is a desert lake that combines beauty with a convenient location. Only a short trip from the interstate, this new recreation spot was once a barren desert popular with off-road vehicles. After completion of the dam in 2003, the reservoir saw a fill to 80 percent capacity and is now beginning to get visitors.

This park is not about serious paddling. I see it as a place to play in your boat and have fun in the water. There are no key destinations or focuses for a paddle trip. Just get in your boat and have a good time. Paddling shouldn't always be serious, and Sand Hollow is for those moments that aren't.

The reservoir has a very large surface area. Open and completely surrounded by the red desert, the water is smooth and warm. The shoreline is sandy and the sky is blue. This is not a complicated place, so it makes a good place to try out a new canoe or kayak, practice rolls, or just mess around.

Of course, having large red-rock areas is a great attraction. There are forms in various areas around the reservoir. However, the most interesting paddling is not across the water, but just off the shore. A large red-rock island is the perfect spot to investigate and play.

The key aspect that makes Sand Hollow well suited to paddling is its design. I am certain in time this will become a major destination for powerboaters. Its open layout makes it exceptionally well suited to those kinds of sports. However, I believe the area around the shore near the rocks will remain a haven for swimming and paddling. If it becomes too crowded, Quail Creek Reservoir is less than 6 miles away.

Sand Hollow is a convenient and lovely place to take your kayak for a day when nothing matters but some sun, some water, and some time in your boat.

GUNLOCK RESERVOIR

County: Washington
LONG/LAT: N37 15.195 W113 46.452
Elevation: 3,531 feet/1,076 meters
Body Type: Reservoir
Difficulty: Easy
Season: Spring, summer, autumn, winter
Size: 266 acres
Directions: From St. George, head west on UT 8 (Sunset Boulevard) through Santa Clara to Shivwits. Take the road going right and go about 5 miles to the reservoir. The reservoir entrance is on the left.

Put-in: There is a boat ramp and pier just inside the park, right below the parking lot. The reservoir also has a fairly smooth shore in areas and could be used for a put-in.

Other Sports: Fishing, camping

Information: www.stateparks.utah.gov/park_pages/parkpage.php?id=glsp

Paddle Overview

While I spend a lot of time on the water during the warm months, I often get a bug to go paddle during the winter season. Sure, skiing is fantastic and I love the snow, but there are times when a good paddle just sounds like the perfect antidote for the winter doldrums. Gunlock Reservoir is the medicine to fix those wintertime blues.

Just west of St. George, Gunlock is available for paddling during all four seasons. The mild winter weather in this region means that the water may be somewhat cool, but not covered in ice. This whole region is a place for people who love to golf during the winter. Why not add paddling to that list of activities?

Gunlock is a lovely place. The water is cerulean blue and glitters in the southern Utah sun. The surrounding area has diverse red rock formations decorated with sage and juniper. It is a high-desert oasis that provides a nice-sized surface area for paddling relatively close to the metropolitan area nearby.

The reservoir resides in a canyon with a range of mountains on either side. The Bull Valley Mountains are to the west, and the Red Mountains are to the east. This position encourages a windy surface, and on my visit this was the case. However, the wind should not be a deterrent to paddling Gunlock.

One feature of the reservoir is the spillways. After heavy rains, the overflow is dumped into the Santa Clara River. The cascading water tumbles over the red rocks, creating a waterfall effect. You are more likely to catch these views in the spring, when the reservoir is high and the rain is more frequent.

A good winter getaway, Gunlock Reservoir

If you want to enjoy the scenery for longer than a day, campsites are available at the reservoir. The beautiful red cliffs interspersed with green foliage and the delightful paddling combine to make Gunlock an appealing destination for a multi-day trip. This is the perfect paddle therapy.

OTHER DESTINATIONS

IVINS RESERVOIR

County: Washington

LONG/LAT: N37 10.708 W113 42.938

Size: Approximately 57 acres

Directions: From St. George, head west on UT 8 (Sunset Boulevard) through Santa Clara to just before Shivwits. If you enter the reservation, you have gone too far. The reservoir is just a little jaunt off the service road. The reservoir entrance is on the right side of the road.

Comment: Ivins is a relatively small and unattractive reservoir with amazing Red Mountain views. The setting really is fantastic, but the water is sort of smelly, and there was a strange muddy wash over the place. It looks like there was a time when the place was treated like a park, but much of it is run down and neglected.

PANGUITCH LAKE

County: Garfield

LONG/LAT: N37 43.252 W112 37.585

Size: 1,248 acres

Directions: From Panguitch, head south on UT 143 for about 17 miles. The road follows along the shore, and there is a variety of marinas and shore access available in the area.

Comment: Panguitch is quite nice, but it is also very popular and littered with fishing boats. Its large size and noted fishing are year-round draws. Paddling is not out of the question, but there are more secluded and interesting spots within driving distance, such as Tropic Reservoir or Pine Lake.

QUAIL CREEK RESERVOIR

County: Washington

LONG/LAT: N37 10.775 W113 23.739

Size: 590 acres

Directions: From St. George, head north on I-15. Take exit 16 (UT 9) and travel east for 2 miles. Turn left onto UT 318 and follow it to the reservoir. There is a view area before you get to the state park.

Comment: Quail Creek was the standard powerboating spot in Washington County until the arrival of Sand Hollow. It has high-plateau scenery and is very epic in its setting. If Sand Hollow lures more people away, there may be good paddling opportunities.

RECAPTURE LAKE

County: San Juan
LONG/LAT: N37 .668056 W109 44.556
Size: 265 acres

Directions: From Blanding, head north on US 191 for about 3miles. The reservoir is located directly off the road.

Comment: This lake is a beautiful paddle in a location so isolated that unless you live in Blanding, it is not really worth the drive. Practically to the Four Corners area of the state, the lake exists down here with little else. However, drop in if you're in the neighborhood.

UPPER ENTERPRISE RESERVOIR

County: Washington
LONG/LAT: N37 31.123 W113 51.537
Size: 265 acres

Directions: From St. George, head north on UT 18 to Enterprise. In Enterprise, take a left and head west on the service road. At Hebron Historical Marker, follow the road south to the Upper reservoir. (There are two reservoirs, Lower and Upper. Lower does not appear to be usable.)

Comment: This reservoir is way out of the way and not very attractive for paddling. It is open and very susceptible to wind. However, it has some nice camping and fascinating rock forms called the

Honeycomb Rocks. These tall and hole-filled rocks will entice children to climb and explore.

WIDE HOLLOW RESERVOIR

County: Garfield

LONG/LAT: N37 47.230 W111 37.826

Size: 145 acres

Directions: From Escalante, take UT 12 west just out of town. As you head west, the reservoir will be on the right side of the road, inside Escalante State Park.

Comment: This is a nice reservoir attached to a state park. It has a good pier and in general looks like a fun place to paddle. The fascinating feature of the location is its proximity to a petrified forest. You can see examples of the petrified wood right by the reservoir, and a short hike will take you into the forest.

Appendix

INTERNET RESOURCES

Mike Fine's (*Author*) Web Site	www.paddlenround.com
Weather	www.accuweather.com
Garmin (*Sponsor*)	www.garmin.com
Paddling Information	www.paddling.net
U.S. Coast Guard Boater Safety	www.uscgboating.org
U.S. Forest Service	www.fs.fed.us
Utah Bureau of Land Management	www.ut.blm.gov
Utah Rivers Council	www.utahrivers.org
Utah State Parks	www.stateparks.utah.gov
Utah Travel and Tourism	www.utah.com
Werner Paddles (*Sponsor*)	www.wernerpaddles.com
Wilderness Systems (*Sponsor*)	www.wildernesssystems.com

MILEAGE CHART

	Beaver	Boulder	Brigham City	Bullfrog	Cedar City	Duchesne	Escalante	Green River	Heber City	Loa
Beaver	0	144	256	289	53	251	113	184	183	115
Boulder	144	0	314	151	148	250	28	140	242	54
Brigham City	256	314	0	355	307	171	369	240	102	261
Bullfrog	289	151	355	0	334	235	179	125	284	133
Cedar City	53	148	307	334	0	303	121	236	235	167
Duchesne	251	250	171	235	303	0	277	118	70	210
Escalante	113	28	369	179	121	277	0	167	297	81
Green River	184	140	240	125	236	118	167	0	167	158
Heber City	183	242	102	284	235	70	297	167	0	189
Loa	115	54	261	133	167	210	81	158	189	0
Logan	280	338	25	379	330	194	392	262	125	284
Manti	109	138	182	235	161	143	164	135	109	83
Moab	235	192	292	172	287	170	219	52	219	210
Nephi	116	175	142	273	168	137	229	174	70	121
Ogden	234	293	25	335	286	150	347	217	80	239
Panguitch	47	94	303	227	67	298	67	200	230	94
Park City	200	260	93	301	253	87	314	184	17	205
Price	181	196	176	180	234	55	223	64	104	156
Provo	155	214	102	256	207	96	268	138	28	160
Richfield	64	100	226	222	115	175	127	123	154	46
Salt Lake	200	258	60	299	250	113	312	182	44	204
St. George	105	212	360	387	53	355	185	288	287	220
Vernal	309	308	229	292	361	58	336	176	128	267

Logan	Manti	Moab	Nephi	Ogden	Panguitch	Park City	Price	Provo	Richfield	Salt Lake	St. George	Vernal
280	109	235	116	234	47	200	181	155	64	200	105	309
338	138	192	175	293	94	260	196	214	100	258	212	308
25	182	292	142	25	303	93	176	102	226	60	360	229
379	235	172	273	335	227	301	180	256	222	299	387	292
330	161	287	168	286	67	253	234	207	115	250	53	361
194	143	170	137	150	298	87	55	96	175	113	355	58
392	164	219	229	347	67	314	223	268	127	312	220	336
262	135	52	174	217	200	184	64	138	123	182	288	176
125	109	219	70	80	230	17	104	28	154	44	287	128
284	83	210	121	239	94	205	156	160	46	204	220	267
0	205	314	165	48	326	116	199	125	249	83	383	252
205	0	188	42	160	125	126	97	81	49	125	213	201
314	188	0	225	269	252	235	115	190	175	234	340	221
165	42	225	0	120	163	87	101	41	86	85	220	195
48	160	269	120	0	281	71	155	81	205	38	338	208
326	125	252	163	281	0	247	198	202	79	246	119	356
116	126	235	87	71	247	0	120	45	171	31	304	145
199	97	115	101	155	198	120	0	75	121	119	286	112
125	81	190	41	81	202	45	75	0	126	45	259	154
249	49	175	86	205	79	171	121	126	0	169	167	233
83	125	234	85	38	246	31	119	45	169	0	303	171
383	213	340	220	338	119	304	286	259	167	303	0	413
252	201	221	195	208	356	145	112	154	233	171	413	0

GOVERNMENT RESOURCES

Utah Offices

Bureau of Land Management
Utah State Office
 440 West 200 South, Suite 500
 Salt Lake City, UT 84101
 801-539-4001 (*phone*), 801-539-4013 (*fax*)

Bureau of Land Management
Mailing Address
 P.O. Box 45155
 Salt Lake City, UT 84145-0155

Utah State Parks
 1594 West North Temple
 Salt Lake City, UT 84114
 801-538-7220

United States Forest Service Offices

Ashley National Forest
 355 North Vernal Avenue
 Vernal, UT 84078
 435-789-1181

Dixie National Forest
 1789 Wedgewood Lane
 Cedar City, UT 84720
 435-865-3700

Fishlake National Forest
 115 East 900 North
 Richfield, UT 84701
 435-896-9233

GOVERNMENT RESOURCES (continued)

Glen Canyon National Recreation Area
P.O. Box 1507
Page, AZ 86040-1507
923-608-6200 (*Headquarters*)
435-684-7400 (*Bullfrog Visitor Center*)

Manti-La Sal National Forest
599 West Price River Drive
Price, UT 84501
435-637-2817

Uinta National Forest
88 West 100 North
P.O. Box 1428
Provo, UT 84601
801-342-5100

Wasatch-Cache National Forest
Recreation Information (*located inside REI*)
3285 East 3300 South
Salt Lake City, UT 84109
801-466-6411
(open Tuesday through Saturday, 10:30 AM–7:00 PM)
Administrative Offices
125 South State Street
Salt Lake City, UT 84138
801-236-3400

DESTINATIONS BY COUNTY

Beaver	Minersville (p. 155)
Box Elder	Bear River Migratory Bird Refuge (p. 45)
	Willard Bay (p. 52)
Cache	Cutler Marsh (p. 48)
	Cutler Reservoir (p. 51)
	Hyrum Reservoir (p. 51)
	Mantua Reservoir (p. 42)
	Newton Reservoir (p. 52)
	Porcupine Reservoir (p. 40)
	Tony Grove (p. 37)
Carbon	Scofield Reservoir (p. 177)
Daggett	Boulger Lake (p. 169)
	Browne Lake (p. 144)
	Flaming Gorge Reservoir (p. 123)
	Sheep Creek Lake (p. 118)
	Spirit Lake (p. 112)
Davis	Great Salt Lake (p. 58)
	Jordan River (p. 69)
Duchesne	Big Sand Wash (p. 99)
	Boreham Lake (Midview Reservoir) (p. 99)
	Butterfly Lake (p. 128)
	Lower Stillwater Ponds (p. 86)
	Mirror Lake (p. 108)
	Moon Lake (p. 83)
	Pass Lake (p. 130)
	Starvation Reservoir (p. 101)
	Twin Pots (p. 102)

DESTINATIONS BY COUNTY (continued)

Emery	Boulger Lake (p. 169)
	CC Pond (p. 169)
	Cleveland Reservoir (p. 172)
	Electric Lake (p. 169)
	Joe's Valley Reservoir (p. 167)
	Huntington Lake (p. 177)
	Miller Flat Reservoir (p. 178)
	Millsite Reservoir (p. 162)
Garfield	Lake Powell (p. 192)
	Lower Bowns Reservoir (Bowns Reservoir, Bounds Reservoir) (p. 185)
	Panguitch Lake (p. 202)
	Pine Lake (p. 189)
	Tropic Reservoir (p. 187)
	Wide Hollow Reservoir (p. 204)
Grand	Green River (p. 164)
Juab	Mona Reservoir (p. 136)
	Yuba Lake (Sevier Bridge Reservoir) (p. 141)
Kane	Lake Powell (p. 192)
	Navajo Lake (p. 195)
Millard	DMAD Reservoir (Delta) (p. 152)
	Scipio Lake (p. 157)
Morgan	East Canyon (p. 78)
	Lost Creek Reservoir (p. 67)
Piute	Otter Creek Reservoir (p. 156)

DESTINATIONS BY COUNTY (continued)

	Piute Reservoir (p. 156)
Rich	Bear Lake (p. 35)
	Birch Creek Reservoir (p. 51)
	Woodruff Creek Reservoir (p. 53)
Salt Lake	Jordan River (p. 69)
	Little Dell Reservoir (p. 72)
San Juan	Lake Powell (p. 192)
	Recapture Lake (p. 203)
Sanpete	9 Mile (p. 152)
	Gunnison Reservoir (p. 154)
	Huntington Reservoir (Mammoth Reservoir) (p. 175)
	Palisades Lake (p. 150)
	Yuba Lake (Sevier Bridge Reservoir) (p. 141)
Sevier	Fish Lake (p. 145)
	Forsyth Reservoir (p. 148)
	Johnson Valley Reservoir (p. 143)
	Koosharem Reservoir (p. 155)
	Mill Meadow (p. 155)
	Redmond Lake (p. 138)
	Rocky Ford Reservoir (p. 157)
Summit	Beaver Lake (p. 127)
	Echo Reservoir (p. 125)
	Hoop Lake (p. 116)
	Lily Lake (p. 128)

DESTINATIONS BY COUNTY (continued)

	Lily Lake #2 (p. 128)
	Lost Lake (p. 129)
	Lyman Lake (p. 129)
	Rockport Reservoir (p. 130)
	Smith and Morehouse Reservoir (p. 121)
	Teapot Lake (p. 128)
	Trial Lake (p. 130)
	Washington Lake (p. 110)
	Whitney Reservoir (p. 131)
Uintah	Bottle Hollow Reservoir (p. 100)
	Bullock Lake (p. 100)
	Calder Reservoir (p. 100)
	Cottonwood Lake (p. 100)
	Crouse Reservoir (p. 101)
	East Park Reservoir (p. 96)
	Matt Warner Reservoir (p. 93)
	Pelican Lake (p. 89)
	Red Fleet Reservoir (p. 91)
	Steinaker Reservoir (p. 102)
Utah	Jordan River (p. 69)
	Utah Lake (p. 79)
Wasatch	Currant Creek Reservoir (p. 77)
	Deer Creek (p. 78)
	Jordanelle Reservoir (p. 78)
	Soldier Creek and Strawberry Reservoir (p. 79)

Washington	Gunlock Reservoir (p. 201)
	Ivins Reservoir (p. 202)
	Kolob Reservoir (p. 183)
	Quail Creek Reservoir (p. 202)
	Sand Hollow Reservoir (p. 197)
	Upper Enterprise Reservoir (p. 203)
Wayne	Mill Meadow (p. 155)
Weber	Causey Reservoir (p. 64)
	Pineview Reservoir (p. 62)
	Weber River (p. 75)

DESTINATION ELEVATIONS

Name	Feet	Meters
Butterfly Lake	10350	3155
Spirit Lake	10159	3096
Pass Lake	10019	3054
Mirror Lake	10000	3048
Washington Lake	9922	3024
Lily Lake and Teapot Lake	9910	3021
Lost Lake	9870	3008
Trial Lake	9637	2937
Hoop Lake	9377	2858
Beaver Lake	9300	2835
Whitney Reservoir	9255	2821
Lyman Lake	9108	2776
East Park Reservoir	8999	2743
Navajo Lake	8995	2742

DESTINATION ELEVATIONS (continued)

Name	Feet	Meters
Huntington Reservoir (Mammoth Reservoir)	8957	2730
Lily Lake #2	8900	2713
Cleveland Reservoir	8823	2689
Johnson Valley Reservoir	8734	2662
Boulger Lake	8732	2662
Fish Lake	8730	2661
CC Pond	8693	2650
Sheep Creek Lake	8624	2629
Electric Lake	8561	2609
Miller Flat Reservoir	8462	2579
Browne Lake	8276	2523
Panguitch Lake	8174	2491
Pine Lake	8103	2470
Tony Grove	8043	2452
Kolob Reservoir	7993	2436
Forsyth Reservoir	7969	2429
Smith and Morehouse Reservoir	7960	2426
Tropic Reservoir	7836	2388
Mill Meadow	7714	2351
Matt Warner Reservoir	7659	2334
Scofield Reservoir	7647	2331
Currant Creek Reservoir	7642	2329
Twin Pots	7611	2320

DESTINATION ELEVATIONS (continued)

Name	Feet	Meters
Moon Lake	7573	2308
Lower Bowns Reservoir (Bowns Reservoir, Bounds Reservoir)	7434	2266
Lower Stillwater Ponds	7410	2259
Calder Reservoir	7289	2222
Soldier Creek and Strawberry Reservoir	7251	2210
Crouse Reservoir	7197	2194
Joe's Valley Reservoir	6996	2132
Koosharem Reservoir	6904	2104
Birch Creek Reservoir	6807	2075
Woodruff Creek Reservoir	6788	2069
Otter Creek Reservoir	6325	1928
Piute Reservoir	6263	1909
Millsite Reservoir	6212	1893
Jordanelle Reservoir	6166	1879
Recapture Lake	6068	1850
Rockport Reservoir	6038	1840
Flaming Gorge Reservoir	6023	1836
Lost Creek Reservoir	6000	1829
Wide Hollow Reservoir	5931	1808
Scipio Lake	5910	1801
Bear Lake	5901	1799
Palisades Lake	5868	1789
Huntington Lake	5839	1780
Big Sand Wash	5833	1778

DESTINATION ELEVATIONS (continued)

Name	Feet	Meters
Little Dell Reservoir	5798	1767
Starvation Reservoir	5793	1766
Utah Lake	5761	1756
Upper Enterprise Reservoir	5744	1751
Red Fleet Reservoir	5735	1748
Causey Reservoir	5698	1737
East Canyon	5690	1734
Steinaker Reservoir	5612	1711
Echo Reservoir	5560	1695
Minersville	5503	1677
9 Mile	5381	1640
Deer Creek	5381	1640
Porcupine Reservoir	5381	1640
Gunnison Reservoir	5375	1638
Boreham Lake (Midview Reservoir)	5282	1610
Cottonwood Lake	5254	1601
Bullock Lake	5254	1601
Rocky Ford Reservoir	5190	1582
Mantua Reservoir	5159	1572
Bottle Hollow	5151	1570
Redmond Lake	5110	1558
Yuba Lake (Sevier Bridge Reservoir)	4954	1510
Pineview Reservoir	4900	1494
Pelican Lake	4848	1478

DESTINATION ELEVATIONS (continued)

Name	Feet	Meters
Newton Reservoir	4778	1456
DMAD Reservoir (Delta Reservoir)	4665	1422
Hyrum Reservoir	4664	1422
Great Salt Lake	4500	1372
Mona Reservoir	4490	1369
Cutler Marsh	4402	1342
Cutler Reservoir	4402	1342
Weber River	4320	1317
Willard Bay	4223	1287
Jordan River	4209	1283
Bear River Migratory Bird Refuge	4205	1282
Green River	4079	1243
Lake Powell	3700	1128
Gunlock Reservoir	3531	1076
Ivins Reservoir	3086	941
Sand Hollow Reservoir	3023	921
Quail Creek Reservoir	2993	912

GPS COORDINATES

9 Mile	N39 10.323 W111 42.348
Bear Lake	N41 53.090 W111 21.806
Bear River Migratory Bird Refuge	N41 28.452 W112 10.629
Beaver Lake	N40 49.609 W110 56.476

GPS COORDINATES (continued)

Big Sand Wash	N40 17.123 W110 13.211
Birch Creek Reservoir	N41 30.461 W111 18.702
Boreham Lake (Midview Reservoir)	N40 10.543 W110 10.468
Bottle Hollow	N40 18.103 W109 52.821
Boulger Lake	N39 38.688 W111 15.254
Browne Lake	N40 51.652 W109 48.697
Bullock Lake	N40 21.151 W109 49.158
Butterfly Lake	N40 43.245 W110 52.092
Calder Reservoir	N40 43.788 W109 12.952
Causey Reservoir	N41 17.448 W111 34.988
CC Pond	N39 39.307 W111 17.787
Cleveland Reservoir	N39 34.928 W111 14.780
Cottonwood Lake	N40 21.218 W109 47.738
Crouse Reservoir	N40 43.574 W109 11.223
Currant Creek Reservoir	N40 20.039 W111 03.041
Cutler Marsh	N41 44.793 W111 57.164
Cutler Reservoir	N41 47.216 W111 57.238
Deer Creek	N40 26.836 W111 28.709
DMAD Reservoir (Delta Reservoir)	N39 39.8333 W112 47.2778
East Canyon	N40 52.726 W111 34.906
East Park Reservoir	N40 46.802 W109 33.141
Echo Reservoir	N40 55.390 W111 24.243
Electric Lake	N39 38.259 W111 14.187
Fish Lake	N38 32.068 W111 44.179
Flaming Gorge Reservoir	N40 54.878 W109 25.663

GPS COORDINATES (continued)

Location	Coordinates
Forsyth Reservoir	N38 31.218 W111 31.706
Great Salt Lake	N41 03.593 W112 14.321
Green River	N38 59.326 W110 09.020
Gunlock Reservoir	N37 15.195 W113 46.452
Gunnison Reservoir	N39 12.370 W111 42.472
Hoop Lake	N40 54.383 W110 03.616
Huntington Lake	N39 20.712 W110 56.425
Huntington Reservoir (Mammoth Reservoir)	N39 35.176 W111 15.630
Hyrum Reservoir	N41 37.688 W111 52.010
Ivins Reservoir	N37 10.708 W113 42.938
Joe's Valley Reservoir	N39 18.051 W111 16.332
Johnson Valley Reservoir	N38 37.133 W111 38.532
Jordan River	N40 43.995 W111 55.402
Jordanelle Reservoir	N40 52.726 W111 34.906
Kolob Reservoir	N37 26.295 W113 02.693
Koosharem Reservoir	N38 35.984 W111 50.797
Lake Powell	N37 30.970 W110 43.680
Lily Lake and Teapot Lake	N40 40.826 W110 56.322
Lily Lake #2	N40 52.740 W110 48.637
Little Dell Reservoir	N40 47.335 W111 40.600
Lost Creek Reservoir	N41 11.070 W111 22.571
Lost Lake	N40 40.818 W110 56.258
Lower Bowns Reservoir (Bowns Reservoir, Bounds Reservoir)	N38 06.330 W111 16.562
Lower Stillwater Ponds	N40 30.646 W110 34.950

GPS COORDINATES (continued)

Lyman Lake	N40 56.465 W110 36.493
Mantua Reservoir	N41 30.177 W111 56.548
Matt Warner Reservoir	N40 46.612 W109 18.235
Mill Meadow	N38 30.931 W111 33.846
Miller Flat Reservoir	N39 34.522 W111 15.386
Millsite Reservoir	N39 05.523 W111 11.687
Minersville	N38 13.103 W112 49.793
Mirror Lake	N40 42.611 W110 53.621
Mona Reservoir	N39 52.521 W111 52.332
Moon Lake	N40 31.209 W110 26.402
Navajo Lake	N37 31.048 W112 45.670
Newton Reservoir	N41 27.928 W111 19.175
Otter Creek Reservoir	N38 10.032 W112 01.052
Palisades Lake	N39 15.321 W111 39.421
Panguitch Lake	N37 43.252 W112 37.585
Pass Lake	N40 42.761 W110 53.633
Pelican Lake	N40 10.932 W109 41.664
Pine Lake	N37 44.587 W111 57.406
Pineview Reservoir	N41 15.848 W111 49.522
Piute Reservoir	N38 19.553 W112 13.125
Porcupine Reservoir	N41 31.010 W111 44.080
Quail Creek Reservoir	N37 10.775 W113 23.739
Recapture Lake	N37 .668056 W109 44.556
Red Fleet Reservoir	N40 35.129 W109 26.526
Redmond Lake	N38 59.900 W111 52.249

GPS COORDINATES (continued)

Rockport Reservoir	N40 45.233 W111 22.446
Rocky Ford Reservoir	N38 52.105 W111 57.400
Sand Hollow Reservoir	N37 07.136 W113 23.006
Scipio Lake	N39 07.279 W112 03.307
Scofield Reservoir	N39 44.982 W111 09.052
Sheep Creek Lake	N40 53.276 W109 50.980
Smith and Morehouse Reservoir	N40 45.310 W110 06.091
Spirit Lake	N40 50.246 W110 00.178
Starvation Reservoir	N40 10.414 W110 29.509
Steinaker Reservoir	N40 30.959 W109 31.509
Soldier Creek and Strawberry Reservoir	N40 10.987 W111 01.653
Tony Grove	N40 .183117 W111 .027550
Trial Lake	N40 40.759 W110 57.359
Tropic Reservoir	N37 36.256 W112 15.373
Twin Pots	N39 20.712 W110 56.425
Upper Enterprise Reservoir	N37 31.123 W113 51.537
Utah Lake	N40 14.105 W111 44.208
Washington Lake	N40 40.814 W110 57.683
Weber River	N41 10.028 W111 59.936
Whitney Reservoir	N40 50.633 W110 55.826
Wide Hollow Reservoir	N37 47.230 W111 37.826
Willard Bay	N41 25.302 W112 03.206
Woodruff Creek Reservoir	N41 27.928 W111 19.175
Yuba Lake (Sevier Bridge Reservoir)	N39 24.247 W112 01.464

Index

A

Alcohol, xxviii–xxix
Altitude sickness, 21
Anasazi ruins, 182
Antelope Island, 58, 59, 61
Arches National Park, 161
Ashley National Forest, 82, 105

B

Bald Mountain, 109
Bear Lake, 34, 35–37
Bear River Migratory Bird Refuge, 45–48
Bear River Range, 39
Beaver, UT, 135
Beaver Creek, 119
Beaver Lake, 127
Big Rock Candy Mountain, 135
Big Sand Wash, 99
Bilge pumps and sponges, 12

Birch Creek Reservoir, 51
Black Mountains, 139
Boats, 9–10
Bonneville Salt Flats, 61–62
Boreham Lake (Midview Reservoir), 99
Bottle Hollow, 100
Boulder, UT, 182
Boulder Mountain, 186
Boulger Lake, 169–72
Bowery Haven Marina, 146
Brigham City, UT, 33, 35
Brigham Young University, 57
Browne Lake, 114–16
Bryce Canyon National Park, 188
Bug spray, 15
Bull Valley Mountains, 200
Bullfrog, UT, 182, 192, 194
Bullock Lake, 100

Bureau of Land Management, 167
Butterfly Lake, 128

C

Cache Valley, 34
Calder Reservoir, 100–101
Capitol Reef National Park, 149, 186
Castle Country Region
  destinations, 158–78
  overview, 18
Cattle guards, xxvi–xxvii
Causey Reservoir, 64–67
CC Pond, 169–72
Cedar Breaks National Monument, 197
Cedar City, UT, 134–35
Cedar Overlook, 160
Cell phones, xxiv
Central Utah Water District, 99
Central Western Region
  destinations, 133–57
  overview, 18
Cleveland Reservoir, 172–74
Cleveland-Lloyd Dinosaur Quarry, 160–61
Climate, xix
Clothing, 14
Coalville, UT, 105, 130
Colorado Plateau, 188
Colorado River, 161, 162, 192
Corrine, UT, 45
Cottonwood Lake, 100

Counties, 20
Crouse Reservoir, 101
Crystal Geyser, 166
Currant Creek Reservoir, 77–78
Cutler Marsh, 48–51
Cutler Reservoir, 51

D

Davis County, 56
Dead Horse Point, 161
Deck towels, 12
Deer Creek, 78
Delta, UT, 135
Desert View Overlook, 149
Destinations
  best bets, 19–29
  other destinations, 29–30
  regional information, 17–19
Diamond Mountain Plateau, 95
Difficulty levels, 23–24
Dinosaur National Monument, 82
Dinosaur Trackway, 92
Directions, 26
Dirty Delta River, 192
Dixie National Forest, 182
DMAD Reservoir (Delta Reservoir), 152–53
Driving in Utah, xxiv–xxvii
Dry bags and boxes, 13
Duchesne, UT, 82
Duchesne County, 81–83
Dutch John, UT, 105, 125

E

East Canyon, 78
East Park Reservoir, 96–98
Echo Reservoir, 125–27
Eden, UT, 64
Egg Island, 61
Electric Lake, 169–72
Elevation, 21
Emigration Canyon, 73
Equipment, 6–15
Escalante, UT, 182

F

Fees and permits, xxx–xxxi
Ferron Canyon, 164
First-aid kits, 8
Fish Creek, 85
Fish Lake, 144, 145–48
Fish Lake Plateau, 144
Fishlake National Forest, 136
Flaming Gorge, 82, 105
Flaming Gorge Reservoir, 123–25
Food, 9
Forsyth Reservoir, 148–50
Fort Buenaventura, 75, 77
Fort Duchesne, UT, 82, 99, 102

G

Garden City, UT, 34
Glen Canyon, 182
Goblin Valley State Park, 161
Gooseberry-Fremont Scenic Backway, 145
GPS (global positioning system), 11–12
Grand County, 161
Grand Staircase Escalante National Monument, 182, 189
Great Salt Lake, 58–62
Green River, 124, 161, 164–67
Green River, UT, 161
Green River State Park, 165, 166
Greenway Trail, 77
Gunlock Reservoir, 199–201
Gunnison Reservoir, 153–54

H

Heber City, UT, 58
Heber Creeper, 58
Hideout Canyon, 124
Hite, UT, 192, 194
Honeycomb Rocks, 204
Hoop Lake, 116–18
Horseshoe Canyon, 124
Huntington, UT, 160, 172
Huntington Canyon, 171, 172, 177
Huntington Lake, 177
Huntington Reservoir (Mammoth Reservoir), 175–77
Huntsville, UT, 64
Hurricane, UT, 181
Hypothermia, 14
Hyrum Reservoir, 51–52

I

Interstate highways, xxii–xxiv
Ivins, UT, 181
Ivins Reservoir, 202

J

Joe's Valley Reservoir, 167–69
Johnson Valley Reservoir, 143–45
Jordan River, 69–72
Jordanelle Reservoir, 78–79

K

Kamas, UT, 106, 130
Kingfisher Island, 124
King's Peak, 103
Kingston Canyon, 156
Kolob Reservoir, 183–85
Koosharem Reservoir, 155

L

Labyrinth Canyon, 161, 166
Lake Powell, 182, 192–94
Lakes, 22–23
Laketown, UT, 34
Larb Hollow Overlook, 187
Launch sites, 26–27
Life jackets, 4–6
Lily Lake, 128
Lily Lake #2, 128–29
Little Bear River, 42
Little Dell Reservoir, 72–74
Little Sahara Recreation Area, 135
Logan, UT, 33–34, 50

Logan Canyon, 34
Logan River, 50
Longitude/latitude, 20–21
Lost Creek Reservoir, 67–69
Lost Lake, 129
Lower Bowns Reservoir (Bowns Reservoir, Bounds Reservoir), 185–87
Lower Stillwater Ponds, 86–88
Lucerne, UT, 123
Lyman Lake, 129

M

Manila, UT, 105–6, 123
Manti, UT, 151–52
Manti-La Sal Mountains, 164
Mantua Reservoir, 42–44
Matt Warner Reservoir, 93–96
Midway, UT, 58
Mill Meadow, 155
Miller Flat Reservoir, 178
Million Dollar Road, 182
Millsite Reservoir, 162–64
Mineral Bottom, 165, 166
Minersville, 155–56
Mirror Lake, 108–10
Mirror Lake Highway, 106–8
Moab, UT, 162
Mona Reservoir, 136–38
Moon Lake, 83–86
Mormons, xxviii, xxix
Mount Nebo, 137
Mustang Ridge, 123

N

Narrows, 181
Native American Nations, xxx
Navajo Lake, 195–97
Nephi, UT, 135
Newton Reservoir, 52
Nine Mile Canyon, 160
9 Mile, 152
Northern Region
  destinations, 33–53
  overview, 18

O

Oakley, UT, 121
Ogden, UT, 56–57
Ogden Canyon, 64
Olympic Park, 106
Orem, UT, 57
Otter Creek Reservoir, 156

P

Paddle Festival, xviii–xix
Paddles, 10–11
Paddling gear, 9–15
Palisades Lake, 150–52
Panguitch, UT, 182
Panguitch Lake, 202
Paradise, UT, 40
Park City, UT, 106
Parley's Canyon, 73
Pass Lake, 130
Pelican Lake, 89–91
Personal flotation devices (PFDs), 4–6
Pine Lake, 189–91
Pineview Reservoir, 62–64
Piute Reservoir, 156–57
Pocketknifes, 7
Porcupine Reservoir, 40–42
Portage, 13
Powell, John Wesley, 124, 167
Price, UT, 160, 175
Price Canyon, 160, 172
Provo, UT, 57
Provo River, 79
Put-ins, 26–27

Q

Quail Creek Reservoir, 202–3

R

Ralston, Aron, xxv
Recapture Lake, 203
Red Canyon, 124, 189
Red Fleet Reservoir, 91–93, 98
Red Mountains, 181, 200
Red Rock Region
  destinations, 179–204
  overview, 18
Redford, Robert, 57–58
Redmond, UT, 140
Redmond Lake, 138–40
Reservoirs, 22
Resorts and lodges

Central Western Region, 135, 147
Red Rock Region, 196
Uinta Range Region, 105, 113, 114
Uintah Basin Region, 85–86
Wasatch Front Region, 57–58
Resource information, 27
Riverdale, UT, 75, 77
Rivers, 23
Rock Cliff Nature Center, 79
Rock Creek, 87
Rockport Reservoir, 130
Rocky Ford Reservoir, 157
Ropes, 6–7
Round Mountains, 85

S

Safety essentials, 6–8
Salina, UT, 140
Salt Lake City, UT, 56
San Rafael Swell, 161
Sand Hollow Reservoir, 197–99
Sanpete Valley, 150
Santa Clara, UT, 181
Santa Clara River, 200
Sardine Canyon, 34–35
Scipio Lake, 157
Scofield Reservoir, 177
Seasons, xix–xxii, 25
Sevier Plateau, 136
Sevier River, 142, 189
Sevier River Valley, 135

Sheep Creek Bay, 123
Sheep Creek Canyon, 124
Sheep Creek Lake, 118–20
Smith and Morehouse Reservoir, 121–23
Soldier Creek, 79
Southern Utah State University, 135
Spirit Lake, 112–14
Spirit Lake Lodge, 113
Spirit Lake Scenic Byway, 112
Springdale, UT, 181
St. George, UT, 181, 200
Starvation Reservoir, 101–2
Steinaker Reservoir, 97, 98, 102
Strawberry Reservoir, 79
Summit County, 105–6
Sundance Film Festival, 57–58
Sundance Resort, 57–58
Sunday store closings, xxix
Sunglasses, sunscreens and hats, 14
Swiss Days, 58

T

Table Cliff Plateau, 191
Teapot Lake, 128
Thanksgiving Point, 57
Timpanogos Cave National Monument, 57
Tony Grove, 37–40
Trial Lake, 111, 130–31
Tropic Reservoir, 187–89

Tuacahn, 181
Twin Pots, 102

U

Uinta Range Region
　destinations, 103–31
　overview, 18
Uintah Basin Region
　destinations, 81–102
　overview, 18
Uintah County, 81–82
Upper Enterprise Reservoir, 203–4
Utah County, 57–58
Utah Lake, 79
Utah Rivers Council, xviii–xix
Utah Shakespearean Festival, 135
Utah State University, 33
Utah's Dixie, 181

V

Valley Mountains, 139
Vernal, UT, 82, 98, 102
Virgin River, 181

W

Wasatch Front Region
　destinations, 55–79
　overview, 18
Wasatch Plateau, 170, 175
Washington, UT, 181
Washington Lake, 110–12
Water
　conservation and management, xvi–xvii
　for drinking, 9
　preservation, xvii
　protection, xvii–xviii
Water Pocket Hollow of Capitol Reef, 187
Weber River, 75–77, 126, 127
Whistles, 6
Whitney Reservoir, 131
Wide Hollow Reservoir, 204
Widgeon Bay, 146
Willard Bay, 52
Woodruff Creek Reservoir, 53

Y

Yellowpine Campground, 88
Young Living Farm, 138
Yuba Lake (Sevier Bridge Reservoir), 141–43

Z

Zion National Park, 181, 184, 185

EU Authorised Representative:
Easy Access System Europe
Mustamäe tee 50, 10621 Tallinn, Estonia

www.ingramcontent.com/pod-product-compliance
Lightning Source LLC
Chambersburg PA
CBHW051423290426
44109CB00016B/1409